WORDLORE

By

DUANE CLAYTON BARNES

E. P. DUTTON & COMPANY, INC.
NEW YORK, 1948

To

PEOPLE

who make and break
our words
this book is dedicated

TABLE OF CONTENTS

WORDLORE

FOREWORD

THIS little volume makes no claim to erudition. There is little in it that anyone with some linguistic background could not dig out of a good dictionary. The book is designed, not for the advanced student of comparative linguistics, but for the general reader — for anyone who has an interest in, and a curiosity about, words.

As a student in school I am afraid I developed little enthusiasm for my English teacher's admonition to "cultivate the dictionary habit." The purpose of this good advice was, of course, to get us to know more accurately the meanings of words by looking up their *definitions*. While I have improved considerably in this respect since my school days, I am even now more interested in the colorful meanings that are to be found, not from current definitions, but rather from the bracketed hieroglyphics that precede dictionary definitions and tell the stories behind words as we know them today. Ever since I developed an interest in foreign languages, the curious derivations of our own words, and the relationships between them, have held a fascination for me.

My desire to share this pleasure with others, and to try to interpret for them in an interesting manner what most consider to be the "dull" information contained within the covers of a dictionary, has prompted the writing of this book. The preparation of it has served only to confirm me in my enthusiasm; if the reading of it sends others scurrying to their dictionaries on word trails of their own, the writing will have been amply justified. The material is by no means exhaustive and leaves plenty of room for further sleuthing.

Because this book is intended for the general reader rather than for the specialist, I have given English translations of all foreign words appearing in the text. A knowledge of foreign languages is by no means essential to an appreciation of word derivation, as long as the meanings of foreign terms are clear. In general, where Latin words occur, I have used the form closest to the English word. There are some simplifications, and some steps have been omitted, but I have sincerely tried to keep the information accurate. Philologists, in common with ordinary mortals, are unable to agree about everything, and some will doubtless object to individual derivations and interpretations. I do not pretend to be an advanced student of linguistics myself and, despite my good intentions, some errors have doubtless crept in. I shall be only too happy to have them pointed out to me.

Many of the examples given could logically have been placed in any one of several chapters. I have tried to put such words where they would be most interesting.

For the information contained in the introductory historical chapter I am indebted very largely, though by no means exclusively, to L. P. Smith's THE ENGLISH LANGUAGE, in the Home University Library series. I hope the reader will not let this chapter scare him away — the succeeding chapters are quite independent of it — but this information about the history of our language, sketchy as it is, should increase the pleasure of what follows.

For derivations and definitions I have depended largely on the excellent WINSTON SIMPLIFIED DICTIONARY, published by the John C. Winston Company of Philadelphia.

I wish here to express my thanks to my wife who gave me great assistance in the preparation of the manuscript.

D. C. B.

Ompah, Ontario

WORDLORE

Chapter I

WAR AND PEACE

THE GERMANS have the expressive word *Wortschatz*, literally "word-treasure," which is infinitely more meaningful than our prosaic "vocabulary." They also say "word-book" for dictionary, "tooth-doctor" for dentist, and "hand-shoe" for glove. But for an accident of history — the Norman Conquest of England under William the Conqueror in 1066 — we should now be speaking such a homespun language ourselves, though it would be closer to modern Dutch than to German. And had it not been for the much earlier invasion of England by the Angles and Saxons, we should even be speaking "British" rather than English (ENGLAND — land of the "Angles"). The native British language was a Celtic tongue allied to modern Welsh and Gaelic. It is a curious fact of history that of this original British speech, only a handful of words survive in English, and some of these are probably later introductions from Irish, Welsh, and the language of Brittany in France.

The two extraordinary features of modern English are: (1) as a result of the Norman invasion, our language has become almost a fifty-fifty mixture of English and French (it has been estimated that about forty-five per cent of our vocabulary is of French origin), and (2) it has become remarkably simplified as regards its grammar. English has lost, for example, nearly all the inflectional endings which cause us so much trouble when we try to learn Latin, German, or even French. In these two respects the language most similar to English is, strange to say, modern Persian. It too suffered an invasion and conquest — by the Arabs — and has received from them a large proportion of its modern vocabulary. Persian has also come nearly as far as English along the path of simplification of its grammar.

We should, however, not regret the fact that we speak a hybrid language, for this very circumstance has enormously increased our "word-treasure" and given us hosts of synonyms with shades of meaning not possessed by other languages. As we shall see later on, many pairs of words which once were identical in meaning have gradually split apart, each one retaining a special nook of its own. Compare, for example, HEARTY and CORDIAL, STOOL and CHAIR, HEAVENLY and CELESTIAL, SHEPHERD and PASTOR.

To show the extent to which we have borrowed from French, let us take a look at two samples of English.[1] First, a few sentences in which there are no words of French origin:

"The might of the Norman hardly made its way into the home of the Saxon, but drew back at the threshold of his house. There, beside the fire in the kitchen [*derived from Latin, but already used in Anglo-Saxon times*] and the hearth in his hall, he met his beloved kindred. The bride, the wife, and the husband, sons and daughters, brothers and sisters tied to each other by love, friendship, and all kindly feelings, knew nothing dearer than their own sweet home. . . ."

And now a passage which is literally teeming with words of French origin:

"To defend his conquest, the Norman gained possession of the country; and, master of the soil, erected fortresses and castles, and attempted to introduce novel terms. The universe and the seasons, the planets and the comets, and even the ocean, attest how much was impressed with the seal of the conqueror. . . . A new splendor was added to society, and foreign customs polished the manners and excited the admiration of the ancient inhabitants, who, charmed by such elegance, recognized in their conquerors persons of a superior intelligence."

It is, of course, significant that, while it is quite possible to write English without using words of French origin, it is out of the question to try to use only words which have come

---

[1] Quoted by Skeat in his "Principles of English Etymology" and taken from the "Outlines of Comparative Philology," by Schele de Vere (with some changes by Skeat.)

to us from French. In spite of his adoption of so many French terms, the Englishman clung to his old familiar words for the things closest to him. The fundamental core of our language still remains Anglo-Saxon.

But though our language today is made up largely of words derived from Teutonic and French sources, we have borrowed many words from every section of the globe, under the influence of war, religion, exploration, trade and commerce. Before we attempt to find the stories behind the words that we use every day, and the extraordinary and unexpected relationships among them, it will be well for us to take a very brief glance at English history, to see not only *where* our words have come from, but *why* they have come to us.

Before we start on this historical jaunt, perhaps a word should be said about the great Indo-European family of languages. It has only been realized in comparatively recent times that languages as different and widespread as English, Scandinavian, German, French, Spanish, Italian, Russian, Polish, Bulgarian, Greek, Latin, Armenian, Persian, and many of the tongues now spoken in India, have all stemmed originally from one common language, and are in fact distant cousins. Of this original common language there are no traces left, but of its existence there can be no doubt. The exact home of this ancient language is only a matter of surmise, but as people gradually wandered off in different directions and settled in different parts of Europe and Asia, each tribe developed its language in its own way, and we have the resulting "confusion of tongues" today. The modern Romance group of languages (French, Spanish, Italian, etc.) has provided a perfect opportunity to trace each back to its source. All the languages of this group are derived directly from Latin, and our knowledge of Latin is very extensive. Unfortunately, we have no such knowledge of the ancestor of the modern Germanic or Teutonic group (German, Dutch, Swedish, etc.). The science of Philology has provided us with sets of fixed rules whereby sound-changes from a parent to a daughter language may be accurately followed or foretold. It is far beyond our scope here to go into this fascinating phase of linguistics, but, as an example, let us take the Latin word *flamma,* flame, and see what happens to the *fl* in French, Spanish, and Italian. In French, *fl* remains intact, and we get the modern French *flamme,* but in Spanish we find *llama,* and in Italian, *fiamma;* and *fl* at the beginning of a Latin word will almost always act this same way in each of those three languages. Compare *cl* in the Romance words for "key": *clef, llave,* and *chiave.* It is not hard to tell to which language each belongs.

Now to get back to Merrie Olde England, or rather to the yet older Britain.

We have noted in passing two great invasions that have profoundly affected our language. But Britain was subjected to other invasions as well, and each has left its mark. First of all came the armies of Caesar, who, having conquered all Gaul, crossed the Channel and extended his dominion to the island of Britain. For upwards of four hundred years, Britain shared the civilization of the Roman Empire, and the Celts of this period even spoke Latin to at least some extent. While most of the Latin borrowings of this time have been lost, we still have a few words of Latin derivation which date from these early times: STREET, for example, from the Latin *strata* (*via*), a paved (road), and WALL, from *vallum.* (Remember that *v* in Latin was pronounced like our *w*.)

Then in the Vth and VIth centuries, we have the invasions of the Angles, Saxons, and Jutes, all Germanic tribes. Here I cannot resist anticipating myself a bit to point out that this ANGLE (and consequently ENGLISH and ENGLAND) is the same word as the ANGLE of ANGLEWORM. This particular tribe came from *Angel,* a "hooked-shaped" district of what is now Schleswig-Holstein. These fierce Germanic invaders found a people far more civilized than themselves, but also considerably

weaker. Wherever they settled in Britain, the Roman civilization, and both the Latin and Celtic languages, disappeared.

At the end of the VIth century came what we might term
a spiritual invasion, with the introduction of Christianity by
St. Augustine, who landed on the island in 597. Christianity
brought with it a revival of learning, and there was again
for a time quite a flourishing civilization. During this period
many Latin words once more came into the language. While
most of these perished in their turn, we still have a few that
were borrowed from Latin during the Anglo-Saxon period.
Many of these words were naturally connected with the
Christian Church: ALTAR, ANGEL, ANTHEM, APOSTLE, BISHOP,
CANDLE, CHURCH, CLERK, CREED, DEACON, DEVIL, DISCIPLE, MAR-
TYR, MONK, NUN, POPE, PRIEST, PSALM, TEMPLE, and several
others. Most of these go back ultimately to Greek, but came in
through the Latin of the Church. Another fairly large group
relates to implements, materials, food, etc.: ANCHOR, BOX,
BUTTER, CHALK, COPPER, CUP, DISH, FORK, INCH, KETTLE, KITCHEN,
MILL, MORTAR, PENNY, PILLOW, PITCH, PLASTER, POUND, SICKLE,
SILK, TILE.

In the VIIIth and IXth centuries, however, another invasion,
this time from Denmark, destroyed a good deal of the civilization which had been fostered by the Christian missionaries.
These new pagan invaders came from a district close to the
homeland of the Angles and Saxons, and the two languages
were so similar as to be easily understood. The races quickly
blended and a mixed language resulted which was mainly
English, but with many Danish words. The Danes contributed
greatly to the simplification of our language, and it was in the
districts where they settled that this process first started.

When we come to the Norman invasion two centuries later,
we find the effect upon our language of quite a different sort.
This was really a third Teutonic invasion, for the Normans
("Northmen") had come originally from Scandinavia, and
were closely related to the Anglo-Saxons and the Danes. But

they had been in France for a hundred and fifty years before crossing the Channel, and had become almost completely assimilated to the French. They had become French in their religion, in their system of law and society, in their manners, and even in their thoughts; so that, for all practical purposes, they came to their English cousins as Frenchmen, and brought with them the speech and civilization of France. They came and remained as conquerors and overlords. For over two centuries their language remained that of the court, of the upper classes, and of the literature of England. English was reduced to the speech of the uneducated peasants. It was no longer taught in the schools, it was no longer used as a literary language, and being freed of the conservative influences of education and culture, it developed very rapidly as a spoken tongue. The two languages, English and Norman French (which, by the way, was only a Norman dialect and different in many ways from the other dialects of France), remained side by side without any considerable intermingling until the XIIIth century. This calls to mind the complaint of the peasant character in *Ivanhoe,* that as long as the animals are alive and have to be tended, they are called PIG, SHEEP, CALF, but when they have been cooked and served before the Norman noblemen, they take on the new-fangled French names PORK, MUTTON, and VEAL!

At the beginning of the XIIIth century (in 1204) the province of Normandy in France was lost to the English Crown, and the English Normans became separated from their French cousins across the Channel. Their speech then developed separately, and many words gradually came to be borrowed from English. This peculiar language is called Anglo-French, and it is from it that most of our French words of this period were borrowed. As time went on, this Anglo-French gradually fell into disuse and English prevailed, but only after having assimilated an enormous proportion of French words. In 1362 English was adopted in the law courts, and shortly after was introduced into the schools. This is the time of Chaucer, and the English of this period is called MIDDLE ENGLISH, as opposed to the earlier OLD ENGLISH of Anglo-Saxon times, and MODERN ENGLISH, dating from the beginning of the XVIIth century.

At this point we must take a little side-trip to find out something of the origins of this language which was introduced to us by the Normans. As we have already seen, French and its sister Romance languages were derived through a gradual evolution of sound changes from ancient Latin. But the great mass of French words came, not from the Latin of Caesar, Cicero, and Virgil, but from the popular, colloquial and spoken Latin of the common people. This Popular Latin was once spoken throughout all the Roman provinces, but it underwent different changes in various regions. Even while it was still Latin, it had become quite different from what we know as Classical Latin. Many of the old words had become changed or even lost, and new ones had been formed. In particular we find a great many new verbs, formed on older Latin roots. One such verb was *duplare,* to double, used instead of the classical *duplicare,* and from which we get the modern French *doubler* (and our English DOUBLE). Other examples of Popular Latin are *battalia,* battle, for the earlier *pugna;* and *caballus,* horse, instead of the classical *equus.* From *caballus* has come the modern French *cheval* (the relationship to the original is more obvious in the Spanish *caballo*). It should be noted that our early Latin borrowings in English come from this same popular source.

A good many Latin words were introduced into both French and English from the Medieval Latin of the Church. This too is rather different from Classical Latin, though it descended from it and retained many of its forms. During the Middle Ages, Latin was a living language, in fact the universal language of European scholars, and continued to be such up to the XVIth century. The borrowings from Medieval Latin were, however, so-called "learned words;" that is, they were brought into the language by scholars and retained in large part their Latin form. More of these learned borrowings occurred later, under the influence of the Renaissance, but this time from Classical Latin sources. In both French and English there are countless pairs of words, derived ultimately from the same Latin word, but quite different in form because the earlier borrowing has undergone a series of popular transformations while its learned cousin has not. The words DOUBLE and DUPLICATE are one example of these doublets. We shall find many more in a later chapter.

The Renaissance brings us back to our main trail again, for we were discussing our borrowings from the French. With the Revival of Learning, the Parisian dialect had become the language of the French court and of French literature, which became very fashionable in England. During this period and the later *Grand Siècle* of the XVIIth century, many more words were adopted from French into English. Up to about 1650 these words were thoroughly naturalized and made to conform pretty much with English spelling and pronunciation. In most borrowings since that time, however, an attempt has been made (with more or less success, depending upon our linguistic abilities!) to pronounce French words *à la française*. A number of words have been borrowed twice, and we get such forms as GENTLE and GENTEEL, GAL'LANT and GALLANT'. This tendency has even given us the modern French spelling of BISCUIT (French for "twice-cooked" — *bis-cuit*), though the word is still pronounced "bisket," as it used to be spelled. How all this irked some Englishmen of the time is shown in the following lines from Samuel Butler's "Satire on Our Ridiculous Imitation of the French:"

> And, while they idly think t'enrich,
> Adulterate their native speech:
> For, though to smatter ends of Greek
> Or Latin, be the rhetorique
> Of pedants counted, and vain-glorious,

To smatter French is meritorious;
And, to forget their mother-tongue,
Or purposely to speak it wrong,
A hopeful sign of parts and wit,
And that they improve and benefit.

With the XVIIth century we come to the period of Modern English and find a language essentially like that which we speak today. Our speech has changed, to be sure, both in vocabulary and pronunciation, and words take on new connotations continually as our ideas and the material things about us are constantly modified from day to day, from year to year, and from century to century. (Think of the new concept behind the word "air-borne" as it is used today.) Thus we must be careful when we read Shakespeare or Milton not to read into their words modern meanings which they did not anticipate.

It now remains to pick up briefly a few scattered elements that have been left by the wayside, other influences that have gone into the making of our every-day speech.

The Greek contribution has not yet been mentioned, but direct borrowing from the Greek was not extensive. By the middle of the XVIth century, Greek was so well known by English and French scholars that they did borrow directly from it, and, of course, in recent times our scientists have borrowed freely from Greek as well as Latin sources (and have even coined words using both languages!) to name their inventions and discoveries. The great bulk of our words from Greek, however, have come to us through Latin which itself abounded in expressions borrowed from this source. Many of these words were taken over into English early enough to have undergone popular transformations just as did similar Latin words. Thus we have, for example, EMERALD, which does not much resemble its Greek forebear *smaragdos*.

We use a good many Italian words in English. While they have come into the language over a long period, and many

have come to us through French, a great many arrived during
the latter half of the XVIth century when it became the fashion
to travel in Italy. (The English have considered Italy pretty
much their own playground ever since.) Our large number
of musical and art terms are too obvious to mention, but to
these we may add many more such as: ALTRUISM, BALCONY,
BELLADONNA, BROCCOLI, CONTRABAND, DILETTANTE, DITTO, EX-
TRAVAGANZA, FIASCO, GRANITE, GROTTO, INCOGNITO, INFLUENZA,
MALARIA, MANIFESTO, MOTTO, QUOTA, STUDIO, UMBRELLA.

Strange to say, a number of native Germanic words have
come to us by the roundabout route of France. There were
Teutonic barbarians serving even in the Roman armies and
some of their words found their way into Latin. Later the
Franks (from which France gets its name), the Goths, and
the Burgundians overran France and added many terms of
war, feudalism, and even sport. Lastly, the Normans brought
a few when they came to France, mostly nautical terms, among
which is our word EQUIP. In all, there are nearly 300 Teutonic
words in English which have come to us through French.
Many of them have changed their original meaning considerably in the course of their wanderings. Among such words we
find BANNER, DANCE, GUARD, GUILE, HARBINGER, HERALD, SKIFF.

Think of the many exotic words we have received from
traders, travellers, pirates, missionaries, etc. One of the early
sources of such words is the Crusades, those fanatical expedi-
tions to the Holy Land which took place in the XIth, XIIth,
and XIIIth centuries. From them we have such words as
ASSASSIN, HAZARD, RENEGADE. These have such interesting
stories behind them that we shall come back to them later.
In the XIIIth and XIVth centuries many such words came to
us through France. Long voyages at sea were at once danger-
ous and difficult, and many articles of commerce from the
East came into England by way of France. An old English
customs list of this period provides us with some interesting
items on which duty had to be paid. While the forms are

generally French, most of the words are easily recognizable: *zucre, alemaunds, argent-vif* (quick-silver), *gingivre, lycorys, spicerie, glasce, figes, reysins, symak* (sumach), *soufre* (sulfur), *yvoire, anys, dates, oille dolive* (olive oil), *gingebred, rys, cotoun.* After the middle of the XVIth century English trade and seamanship developed rapidly and the foundations of the Empire were laid. New foreign terms then came from all over the world, some brought directly by English sailors, and some through the speech of Portuguese, Spanish, and Dutch sailors who had preceded the Englishmen in faraway countries of the globe. From the Far East we have such words as BAMBOO, BANTAM, COOLIE, CURRY, GONG, KOWTOW, TEA, TABOO; from the Near East: COFFEE, DERVISH, HAREM, MAGAZINE, SACK; from Africa: CANARY, CHIMPANZEE, GORILLA; from Latin America: ALLIGATOR, BARBECUE, CANNIBAL, CANOE, CHOCOLATE, COCOA, HAMMOCK, HURRICANE, POTATO, QUININE, TAPIOCA, TOBACCO, TOMATO; and from North America: CAUCUS, HOMINY, MOOSE, RACCOON, SKUNK, as well as many other Indian words too obvious to mention.

Finally, some mention should be made of the great influence exerted upon our language by our men of letters. Chaucer, Wycliffe, and Caxton had no small share in determining that our standard English should be from the dialect spoken in southwestern England rather than from some other dialect which might have given us quite a different mode of speech. All of our great authors have exercised a considerable influence upon the language, though we come back to the hen-and-egg enigma when we try to ascertain just how much they have themselves added to our store and how much they have reflected the speech about them. Milton contains many new words (INFINITUDE, ENSANGUINED, IRRADIANCE, MOONSTRUCK, SATANIC, among others), and Shakespeare's plays have more new words than almost all the other English poets combined (MULTITUDINOUS, INAUSPICIOUS, CLOUD-CAP'T). Spenser revived many old-fashioned and obsolete words, as did Sir Walter Scott and the Romantic movement (RAID, FORAY, BLUFF, GRUESOME, GLAMOUR).

As a result of all these factors which have been at work on our language throughout the centuries of its development, we have at our command the richest storehouse of words (and the largest dictionaries) in the world. In the following chapters we shall look more closely at some of these words which for one reason or another are of particular interest.

Chapter II

A COMEDY OF ERRORS

HAVE you ever wondered what the words "gooseberry" and "mongoose" have to do with a goose? or why a "demijohn" is "half-a-John"? or what connection there may be between a "salt cellar" and a hole in the ground? The answer is that in each case there is no relationship at all. Modern English has many words that have come about accidentally, or through misunderstandings, or from attempts to give a familiar ring to strange words. Some of these do not make sense until we track them down.

Many of these words, like those mentioned above, have come to us in the first place from foreign languages. Sometimes an imported term has sounded like an English word and sometimes a poor attempt at pronouncing a foreign word has reminded us of a native expression. Thus GOOSEBERRY comes from an older form "groseberry," formed on the French word *groseille*. MONGOOSE is from the East Indian *mangus*, the native name for this ferret-like animal. (The word FERRET is interesting in itself, for it comes from the French *furet*, derived ultimately from the Latin *furo,* robber. Our verb to FERRET arises from the use of this type of weasel to "ferret out" rabbits in hunting. MOUSE also stems from an old root meaning "to steal.")

DEMIJOHN has no connection whatever with the "demi-" of "demi-tasse." The word probably comes from the French *dame-jeanne,* "Dame Jane," and possibly originated in fun, with reference to its shape. When the pronunciation was anglicized to "dame-john," these two words made a ridiculous combination, and the first part was eventually assimilated to the prefix "demi-."

Our word SALT CELLAR really means a "salt salt-dish." The second element of the expression was once spelled "saler," and is the French *salière,* salt dish, from Latin *sal,* salt. The idea of "salt" in the word "saler" was finally lost, and so we get the modern compound with a spelling quite unrelated to the original word. Other related words are: SALARY, once a soldier's "salt money" (we still speak of a shiftless individual as "not worth his salt"), and SAUCE and SAUSAGE, which are from the Latin adjective *salsa,* salted. The Italian word for "sauce" or "gravy" is still *salsa.* (The shift from *l* to *u* is typical of modern French. Compare OUTRAGE, now spelled alike in both English and French, with the Old French form *ultrage,* from Latin *ultra,* beyond.)

SIRLOIN has led to the fanciful tale of how an English king, in a fit of good humor at seeing a nice juicy steak placed before him, knighted the steak as "Sir Loin"! Actually, the first half of this word is only a corruption of the French *sur,* on, over, and refers to that part of the flesh that is "over the loin."

I used to wonder about the curious name for the disease SHINGLES. The word is a corruption of the Old French *cengle,* from Latin *cingulum,* a girdle. This very painful ailment causes eruptions to spread around the body like a "girdle." The adjective SUCCINCT is from this same root, though at first glance any connection is hard to see. SUCCINCT is from the Latin *succinctus*, girded, but the verb *suc* (*sub-*) *cingere* (literally, "to gird from below") had the meaning of "to tuck up"into a belt or girdle, and so arose the idea of"compactness."

Why ROSEMARY for a seasoning? Here we have a popular formation, based on the Latin *ros marinus*, marine dew, the name of the aromatic shrub from which we get the seasoning. Both French and German still show the original form, and we find it in Kreisler's "Schön Rosmarin."

The JERUSALEM artichoke certainly did not come from Jerusalem, but that is the best somebody could do with the Italian word *girasole*, which means "turning toward the sun." This name was applied to the plant because it is a member of the sunflower family. ARTICHOKE itself has nothing to do with the word "choke," but is a corruption of the Italian *articiocco*, from the Arabic *al kharshuf*, the artichoke.

"To sleep like a TOP" makes more sense when we know that the phrase is only a bad attempt to translate the French *dormir comme une taupe*, "to sleep like a mole."

And what about WISEACRE? This again is a corruption of the Dutch *wijsegger*, "wise-sayer," from the German *Weis-sager*, soothsayer.

Another word of Dutch origin is FILIBUSTER. The Dutch form is *vrijbuiter* and we have the translation of it in our word FREEBOOTER. From the sense of "pirate" or "robber" the word came to mean someone who "robs" a lawmaking body of its time, and later referred to the act itself.

The expression FORLORN HOPE is perhaps the best disguised, since it has little to do with either "forlorn" (in the modern sense) or "hope." The original Dutch phrase, from which this term is derived, was *verloren hoop*, meaning "lost troop" (the Dutch *hoop* is pronounced "hope" and is related to our HEAP, which once meant "crowd"). The expression was applied to a body of soldiers detached for some service of great danger (the English dictionary gives this as one definition of "forlorn hope" and the idea of a "hopeless" undertaking is implicit in the phrase.

Other foreign words that we have taken over and naturalized are: SEERSUCKER, a corruption of the Persian *shiro shakkar*, a striped garment (literally "milk and sugar"); MUSHROOM, from the French *mousseron* (probably from *mousse*, moss); CRAYFISH or CRAWFISH, for the earlier "crevesse," from the Old French *crevice*, which in turn went back to an old German word *crebig*, crayfish; and MOHAIR, from the Arabic *mukhayyar*, an adjective meaning "choice." The word does refer to hair all right, but not to the hair of a "mo"! Curiously enough, the word MOIRE, watered silk, which we have borrowed from French, is actually a French corruption of the English MOHAIR.

In some cases our attempts to pronounce foreign words have resulted in absolute nonsense. Such a word is the slang term HOOSEGOW, from the Spanish *juzgado*, court, a place where matters are "judged." As a matter of fact, however, HOOSEGOW is a fairly accurate pronunciation of this Spanish word, for the Spanish *j* resembles our *h*, the *z* is coming to have the sound of *s*, and the *d* has all but disappeared. Another nonsense term is HODGEPODGE, which comes from the French *hochepot*, hash (literally, "shake-pot"). Still other examples are: DANDELION, from the French *dent de lion*, lion's tooth (from the shape of the leaf); CURFEW, from the Old French *covrefeu*, "cover-fire" (formerly a warning to put out fires and lights); and JEOPARDY, an English rendering of the Old French *jeu parti*, "divided game" (if you gamble you are in JEOPARDY of losing your stakes). TWEEZERS is another form of the word "tweeze," a case of instruments used by a surgeon. TWEEZERS later came to be applied to one of the instruments in the case. An earlier form is "etweeze," which came from the plural of the French *étui*, case. The word REDINGOTE, a type of coat worn by women, has come from French and shows that the French too have their troubles in trying to pronounce foreign words. REDINGOTE is nothing but a French version of the English "riding coat," which has thus travelled back and forth across the Channel.

NINCOMPOOP and HOCUS-POCUS are presumed to be corruptions of the Latin phrases *non compos (mentis)*, not in possession (of one's mind), and *hoc est corpus (meum)*, "this is (My) body," from the words in the Mass. The latter expression dates from the time of the Reformation, when all things relating to the Catholic Church were anathema. PATTER has a similar derivation. This word comes from *pater (noster)*, "(our) Father," and refers to the rapid and mechanical manner of repeating Latin prayers. Another curious perversion of a Latin phrase occurs in PUNCH AND JUDY, from *Pontius cum Judaeis,* "Pontius (Pilate) with the Jews." This is a relic of an old mystery play taken from St. Matthew xxvii. 19, where Pontius Pilate asks the Jews whom he should release, Barabbas or Jesus. On the other hand, we have the word CONFABULATE and its abbreviated form CONFAB. This is certainly a colloquialism if not a slang term and might appear to be in a class with the others. As far as its ancestry and derivation are concerned, however, CONFABULATE is a perfectly sedate word, stemming from the Latin *confabulari,* to talk together. This verb in turn was formed on the noun *fabula,* tale, FABLE.

In both England and North America, French proper names have been curiously mutilated. Among family names, *St. Paul* becomes SAMPLE or SEMPLE, *St. Denis* changes to SIDNEY, *St. Claire* is SINCLAIR, and *St. Pierre* evolves into SAMPIER. *La Morte Mer* is anglicized into MORTIMER, *Belle Chère* into BELCHER, *Beauchamp* into BEECHAM, *Le Dispensier* (steward) into SPENCER, and *Le Gros Veneur* (great hunter) into GROS-VENOR. BUNKER (Hill) derives from the French *Boncoeur,* the English ROTTEN ROW was once *Route du Roi,* and SHOTOVER is a corruption of *Château Vert* (despite the legendary tale of the prowess of someone's ancestor in "shooting over" a hill). Along the Ottawa River in Canada we find such place names as THE SNOWS, from *Les Chéneaux* (The Channels), THE

SHAWS, from *Les Chats*, and THE SWASHINGS, from *Les Joaquins*. Newfoundland has some really hilarious examples: *Baie de Boules* has lost its reference to "boulders" in BAY BULL, *Rencontre* becomes ROUND COUNTER, *Cinq Iles* is canonized as ST. KEELS, while *Peignoir* gets the worst of it in PINWARE. *Blomidon* takes on a jaunty air as BLOW-ME-DOWN, *Lance-au-Diable* (Devil's Lance) becomes NANCY JOBBLE, and *Baie d'Espoir* (Bay of Hope) belies the optimism of its discoverers with BAY DESPAIR!

There are many English words and words of Anglo-Saxon origin that have been strangely altered. Have you ever connected BEDLAM with "Bethlehem" or MAUDLIN with "Magdalene"? BEDLAM quite understandably comes from the Hospital of St. Mary of "Bethlehem," a London institution for the insane. MAUDLIN is a corruption of St. Mary "Magdalene" (an earlier form was "Maudeleyne"), the first sense being "shedding tears of penitence." The word has come to mean "sloppily sentimental" and then "drunkenly befuddled." SHAMEFACED has been substituted for the earlier "shamefast," formed in the same manner as "steadfast." This change has even affected the meaning of the word, for "shamefast" meant only "modest." Other such corruptions are SCRIMMAGE for "skirmish," and SEXTON for "sacristan." RIGMAROLE has quite a history, and derives from the words "ragman roll." These do not make much more sense unless we know the origin of the expression. "Ragman roll" was the name of an old parlor game. A series of nonsense rhymes was written on a scroll of paper and opposite each verse was affixed a seal with a string attached. When the scroll was rolled up the strings hung down below like so many "rags," so it was a "ragman roll." Each person then took hold of a string and in this way blindly selected a rhyme to read aloud.

Frequently a familiar word is substituted for an unfamiliar one which it more or less resembles. We have already had examples, such as JERUSALEM artiCHOKE. The colloquial SPAR-

ROW GRASS is used for "asparagus," and up in the backwoods
of Ontario, where I have a summer home, the word is shortened to SPAR GRASS. Similarly, because farmers use the expression "tame hay," as opposed to "wild hay," the kind of grass
known as "timothy" has become TAME HAY. Countryfolk now
CORK the seams of a boat, instead of "calking" them. This
transfer is quite understandable, since a CORK is a "stopper."
There is, however, another word "calk" which refers to the
pointed pieces of metal projecting downward from the front
and back of horseshoes. The confusion has extended to this
latter word and farmers now speak of the CORKS on their
horseshoes. For years as a boy I thought of "coleslaw" as
COLDSLAW. Evidently others have been under the same mis-
conception, for you will find this form as an alternate spelling
in the dictionary. "Cole" is derived from the Latin *caulis,*
cabbage (compare CAULIFLOWER, once spelled "collyflory"),
and "slaw" is a Dutch corruption of the French *salade.* If we
would just say "cabbage salad," we would all know what we
were talking about. Another interesting word that I have
heard in Ontario is MAD-AX, for "mattock." In case you do
not own one, a mattock is a glorified PICKAX, which is itself
a corruption of the French *picois.* The idea of "ax" is easily
transferred to these implements because they have an ax-like
handle and are swung much like an ax.

HANGNAIL, TITMOUSE and MEALY-MOUTHED all stem from
Old English words whose original meaning and form we have
lost. HANGNAIL is from the earlier "agnail," formed from the
Anglo-Saxon words *ang,* painful, and *nægl,* nail (compare the
German *Angst,* pain, and *Nagel,* nail). TITMOUSE (a name
for the chickadee), for the earlier "titmose," is really a dupli-
cation. Both "tit" and "mose" meant a small bird. MEALY-
MOUTHED does not mean "with a mouth full of meal," but is
related to such words as MILDEW, MELLIFLUENT and MOLASSES.
MEALY-MOUTHED was once spelled "mele-mouthed" and meant
"honey-mouthed." From the idea of using sweet words came

that of fearing to use plain language. MILDEW is the Old English "meledeaw," honey-dew; but don't ask for a MILDEW when you want a "honey-dew"! The word has suffered a curious shift in meaning. The other two words mentioned come from the related Latin *mel*, honey: MELLIFLUENT means "honey-flowing" and MOLASSES, "honey-like." The latter word came to us through the Portuguese *melaço*, from a Popular Latin *mellaceum*, honey-like (compare the French *miel*, honey).

The word HELPMATE at least makes some sense. It is, however, a corruption of HELPMEET, which never did make sense and is actually not a word at all. This expression arose from an incorrect reading of Genesis II: 18: "I will make him an help meet [*suitable*] for him." The two words were taken for one, with the sense of "helper" or "companion."

Would you believe that GLAMOUR and GRAMMAR were once the same word? GLAMOUR was introduced from Scotch into English by Sir Walter Scott and is derived from the old "grammerye," the study of GRAMMAR, referring specifically in the Middle Ages to Latin grammar. In simple minds the word acquired the meaning of "magic," since Latin was beyond their ken. The word has lost the idea of "magic" today, but a GLAMOUR girl is supposedly one of "magical" beauty. We now use "Greek" almost interchangeably with "magic" when we say "It's all Greek to me."

Now we can settle, at least etymologically, the dispute between Welsh RAREBIT and RABBIT, as well as that between CATSUP, CATCHUP and KETCHUP. RABBIT was unquestionably the original form, and the phrase "Welsh RABBIT" was evidently formed in fun, much like "Spanish woodcock," another cheese dish. Someone without a sense of humor decided that the RABBIT must be a corruption of RAREBIT, which made more culinary sense. (This discussion calls to mind the expression "French leave" — the French say *filer à l'anglaise*, to take English leave!) As for CATSUP, etc., the word is derived from the Malay *kechap,* so KETCHUP is the closest to the original. CATSUP must have been invented by some *grande dame* who felt that CATCHUP was too plebian.

Many expressions have been so changed that we no longer recognize the component parts. AKIMBO is from an old phrase "in kene bowe," meaning "in a sharp (*keen*) bend." LACKA-DAISICAL springs from the archaic exclamation "alack-a-day." WILLY-NILLY was originally "will he nill (*not will*) he." The proper names STEWART and HOWARD had lowly beginnings in "sty-ward" and "hog-ward" respectively (ward = warden, keeper). "Sty" referred to any kind of animal pen, and since he was in charge of the animals, the "steward" became responsible for the food of the house. Similarly, HAYWARD was the "hay-ward," GODDARD the "goat-ward" and STODDARD the "stud-ward," while the BUTLER was once the "bottler" or wine steward.

Other words whose origins are more or less obscured are: DAISY (day's eye), WINDOW (wind-eye, from the Old Norse *vindauga* — compare the German *Auge,* eye), CURTSY (court-esy), FORTNIGHT (fourteen-nights), DOFF (do-off) and its counterpart DON (do-on). In the words DISEASE, PINAFORE, and POTASH the parts have not been obscured other than in our thinking. They mean exactly what they say: "dis-ease" (absence of ease), "pin-afore" (*i.e.,* pinned in front), and "pot-ash" (ashes left in the pot). CHRISTMAS likewise means "Christ's Mass" or Christ's festival.

We have another group of words which are not popular formations or corruptions, but that are not what they may seem at first glance. What do we mean when we say we "don't care a RAP"? This word has nothing to do with knocking, but is the name of an old XVIIIth century Irish counterfeit half-penny. The original sense has long been forgotten. In much the same way the phrase "not worth a CONTINENTAL" refers to worthless money of Revolutionary days. The expression SCOT-FREE may seem reasonable enough when we see the words "Scot" and "free" together! The trouble is that this "scot" was never capitalized. The word comes from the Old French *escot* and means "tax." The original meaning of SCOT-FREE was, then, "free from scot," "untaxed." The noun FORE-BEAR has no connection with the verb "to bear," but is really "fore be-er," "one who *is* before." TURKOMAN bears no relationship to the word "man," but is from the Persian *turkuman,* one like a Turk. The ending -*man* of this word comes from the verb *mandan,* to resemble. The "man" in WOMAN, on the other hand, came about from the generalized use of the word, with the sense of "person," as in "mankind." The Anglo-Saxon form of WOMAN was first *wifmann* and then *wimman,* literally, "a wife (*i.e.,* woman) person." LOOPHOLE is not compounded with our word "loop," but stems from an archaic "loupe," a French word meaning " a narrow window." (In modern French *loupe* has come to mean "magnifying glass.") NIGHTMARE does not necessarily mean that you see wild horses in your dreams. This is the old Anglo-Saxon *mare,* an evil spirit. IRONY's resemblance to "iron" is purely accidental. Here we have the Greek word *eironeia,* pretended ignorance. LIVELONG is really "lief-long" (lief = dear), so the expression "the livelong day" means "the dear long day." The Germans use this identical phrase: *den lieben langen Tag.* SURROUND does not contain the word "round" any more than "bound" is to be seen in ABOUND. The ending "-ound" of both words is ultimately from the Latin verb *undare,* to overflow (literally, "to rise in waves"), from which we also get INUNDATE. The Bible tells of "a land *flowing* [*i.e.,* abounding] with milk and honey."

A FOOTPAD is a robber but the word does not imply that he goes around with his feet wrapped in cloths to avoid making a noise. "Pad" meant originally "highwayman" and is the Dutch word for "path." We find the same word again in PADLOCK, a lock to keep out robbers.

Have you ever wondered why there should be anything

especially mournful about a SADIRON? This is an obsolete "sad," which meant "heavy." MIDWIFE also contains an obsolete word that we no longer understand. This is not the "mid" of "midyear," but is rather an old Anglo-Saxon *mid* which meant "with," the same word as the German *mit*. The -SHIP of such words as "friendship" was once the same word as "shape." The idea behind "friendship" is the "shaping" or state of being a friend.

We find other confusing words in idiomatic phrases that have come down to us from the past. "HUE and cry" has no connection with the "hues" of the sunset. This expression is the Old French *hue et cri,* noise and clamor. Nor can you hang your hat on a "RACK and ruin." RACK is only another form of "wreck" and meant "destruction." "Without LET or hindrance" does not make sense until we know that this LET is the old Anglo-Saxon *lettan,* to hinder, and is actually the same word as "late." The original meaning was "slow." If you are "slow," you make someone else "late" and thus "hinder" him from doing something. "Time and TIDE" does not refer to the periodic ebb and flow of the ocean (although in this case it is the same word), but is the Anglo-Saxon *tid,* time, hour, season. Shakespeare uses the word thus when he says: "There is a TIDE in the affairs of men." We have it again in EasterTIDE, ChristmasTIDE, etc. Even TIDY goes back to the same word and, at the time of Chaucer, meant "timely." "A pig in a POKE" is still understood by many people, for this word POKE is in use in some sections of the country. Some of us, however, do not know that POKE means "bag" and that a POCKET is a "little bag." "As TITE as he can go" is sometimes written "tight," showing that there has been confusion between these two words. TITE derives from an old Scandinavian word meaning "quickly."

Such idiomatic phrases bring to mind another group of words that are relics of the past. These do not lead to mis-interpretation but the original sense has long been forgotten.

Some words remain to us only in idiomatic phrases: "at one FELL swoop" (from Old French *fel,* cruel, barbarous — FELON is from the same source); "might and MAIN" (formerly a noun meaning "strength" — our adjective "main" comes from this old noun); "KITH and KIN" (KITH used to mean "friends" or "neighbors" and of course we have KIN in "kinsman," "kinsfolk," "kindred"). Those who play cribbage should understand the expression "to leave in the LURCH." In this game, if the winner scores 121 before his opponent gets 61, it is a LURCH, and the opponent is "left in the LURCH," *i.e.,* in a difficult or embarrassing position. The word is from an old French game called *lourche.* Has the phrase "to make the WELKIN ring" ever made sense to you? This is an ancient word meaning "clouds" and is the same as the German *Wolken.* The sense of the phrase then is "to make the heavens ring."

There are many more "word relics" that we use without being conscious of the original meaning. If you have ever used NEAT's foot oil on your ski boots, you may have wondered what sort of an animal a NEAT was. The answer is that a NEAT is a cow! This is an old word that meant "cattle" as distinguished from other animals. The oil is made from the feet and shin bones of cattle and calves.

When we speak of a COBWEB, we are using an abbreviation of the ancient word "attercop" (spider) which seems to have meant "poison cup." SPIDER itself is only another form of "spinner," just as SPINSTER is an older feminine of the same word. While we are on the subject of spinning, we may note DISTAFF, formed from the Anglo-Saxon noun *dis,* a bunch of flax. A DISTAFF is a staff from which flax or wool is drawn in spinning. The same *dis* shows up again in BEDIZEN, which once meant only "to dress in linen." BEDIZEN now means "to deck out in finery" and the word DECK has undergone a similar shift in meaning, for it once meant only "to cover." This is still the sense of the word when we speak of the DECK of a boat. Returning for a moment to SPINSTER, we may note that this -*ster* was the regular feminine ending corresponding to the masculine -*er* of "baker." In early days, wars were so frequent that women held most of the jobs. When men did take them over, they often inherited the feminine name for the job, and so we get TEAMSTER and HUCKSTER as well as the proper names WEBSTER and BREWSTER, which have their counterparts in WEBBER (weaver) and BREWER.

A HENCHMAN is really a "horseman" and comes from the Anglo-Saxon *hengest,* horse. The word MARSHAL, now used as a high military rank, had a lowly beginning as "horse servant." MARSHAL came to us through the French *maréchal* from an Old German word *marahscalh* (compare our word "mare"). The subject of horses brings up HOBBYHORSE. This HOBBY comes from an earlier "hoby" or "hobin," a corruption of "Robin," a farmer's pet name for a horse (compare "Dobbin"). From meaning a plaything, the word came to have the sense of a favorite pursuit or pastime, a HOBBY.

A CHAP was once a "peddler," and the word is an abbreviation of CHAPMAN. The old form of this word was "ceapman" and meant "merchant." "Ceap" was a noun meaning "bargain," and from it we have our adjective CHEAP. HUSBAND and HUSSY have both lost their association with "house," but the former used to mean (alas, no longer!) "the master of the house," and the latter is a contraction of "housewife." A SOOTHSAYER was once supposed to be a "truthsayer." We find the same word in Shakespeare's "forsooth." Our coins are now MINTED at the MINT, but this word once had a much less restricted usage. MINT is the Anglo-Saxon *mynet,* coin, and was imported at the time of the Roman invasion of Britain, from the Latin word *moneta.* From this Latin word we also get MONEY, through the Old French *moneie.* (In modern French *monnaie* is still used for "small change," but *argent,* silver, has come to be used for "money.") Even the Latin *moneta* had come to mean MINT, for it was in the Temple of the Goddess Moneta that the Roman money was MINTED.

The adjective MONETARY comes directly from the Latin, and even such words as ADMONISH and SUMMON are related. The last two have, of course, no connection with MONEY, but take us back to the naming of this Roman goddess. According to legend, the sacred geese in the Temple of Juno once cackled a warning of approaching armies, thus giving time for counter-measures, and the goddess was thereafter called *Juno Moneta,* "Juno the Warner," from the verb *monere,* to warn.

The MEAL of PIECEMEAL is really the same word that we find in the phrase "three MEALS a day," which once meant only "three *times* a day." MEAL is the Anglo-Saxon *mæl* or *mal,* which meant both "time" and "mark" (compare the German *einmal,* "one time," and *Denkmal,* memorial, literally "think-marker"). Our modern use of MEAL has arisen from the idea of "mealtime." Indeed the Germans have gone us one better and say "mealtime" (*Mahlzeit*) for MEAL! PIECEMEAL, of course, means "a piece at a *time,*" and we once had many other such compounds: YEARMEAL, DROPMEAL, PENNYMEAL, INCHMEAL, etc.

The word MIDRIFF is another compound, the sense of which has been lost. *Rif* or *hrif* was Anglo-Saxon for "belly." Properly speaking, MIDRIFF is now an anatomical term equivalent to "diaphragm." PENKNIFE is easily understood, if we recall that a small knife was once used to sharpen quill "pens." A HOME-STEAD is really a home "place." We have the word in such phrases as "in STEAD of" and "in my STEAD," and it also occurs in place names like HEMPSTEAD.

This name recalls the old English ditty:

> In ford, in ham, in ley, and tun
> The most of English surnames run.

We may add to our reliquary these old endings, and others as well, still found in many English and American place names. The ending -FORD, in Oxford and Bradford, is the same word as the noun "ford," a place where a stream may be crossed in shallow water. This word derives from the Anglo-Saxon *faran,* to travel, to FARE, preserved in FAREWELL and THOROUGHFARE. I spent my boyhood in the little town of Richford ("Rich's ford"), Vermont. The -HAM of Birmingham, Buckingham, Waltham, and Gotham, is the Anglo-Saxon *ham,* house, HOME, village, HAMLET (which came to us, however, from the related German *Heim,* by way of France). The town of Epsom in Surrey was named "Ebba's Home," after Ebba, the first Christian Queen of England. Berkley, Henley, Wellesley, and Wheatley show the Anglo-Saxon *leah,* meadow, LEA. When we come to -TUN, we have the variants -TON and -TOWN, and all three go back to Anglo-Saxon *tun,* which meant originally "hedge" (compare the German *Zaun,* hedge), then, "an enclosed space," "a group of buildings," a TOWN. These endings show up in such names as Tunbridge, Boston, Middletown. The -DUN, -DEN, and -DOWNE of Dunbar, Dumbarton Oaks, Malden, Hampden, and Landsdowne, are all from the Anglo-Saxon *dun,* hill (see DOWN, page 87). Such names as Newburg, Atterbury ("at-the-bury" — Attleboro is a corruption of the same name), and Scarborough show the variants -BURG, -BURY, and -BOROUGH, which take us back to the Anglo-Saxon *burg,* and its dative form *byrig,* a walled place, a fortress (we find the same word in the old German hymn *Ein Feste Burg,* "A Mighty Fortress"). The form BOROUGH is still used as a separate word. Related to this last group is the ending -BY of Derby, Whitby, and Rugby. Here we have the Old Norse word *byr,* farm, village, town, which has also given us BYLAW. In the same way, the -THORPE of Oglethorpe is an old Anglo-Saxon word for "village." Words like Hampshire, Middlesex, and Norfolk are from old names given to districts in England. The -SHIRE of Hampshire is the Anglo-Saxon *scir,* district, which has given us SHERIFF, a "district" officer of the peace. MIDDLE-SEX was the land of the "Middle Saxons," just as ESSEX was that of the "East Saxons," while WESSEX belonged to the "West

Saxons." NORFOLK was the land of the "North Folk" and SUFFOLK that of the "South Folk."

Some of these endings of town names, however, have come from Latin words, introduced very early into Anglo-Saxon. -WICK and -WICH were the Anglo-Saxon *wic,* borrowed from the Latin *vicus,* village, and have given us such names as Warwick, Chiswick, Greenwich, and Sandwich. BAILIWICK has the same origin and meant "the district under the jurisdiction of a bailiff." The Latin *castrum,* fort, gave us Lancaster, Gloucester, and Manchester, just as *stratum,* street, gave Stratford, and *colonia,* colony, produced Lincoln (as well as the German city of Cologne).

The words NEAR and NEXT are likewise relics of the past. They once formed the comparison "nigh, near, next" and are really "nigher" and "nighest." RATHER is all that remains of the earlier "rathe, rather, rathest," meaning "soon, sooner, soonest."

Some of our verb forms have been "lost in the shuffle." UNCOUTH once meant "unknowing" and is from "couth," the old past participle of the verb "can," which first meant "to know," then "to know how," and finally, "to be able." The Germans still have this verb intact and can say "I have could," where we must use the roundabout form "I have been able." Similarly, we have lost all but the present of MUST, while a German can still say "I have musted." RECKLESS means "heedless" and is all that remains of the archaic verb "to reck." BEQUEATH was formed from an old verb "to quethe," of which we still find the obsolete past "quoth." In primitive times lands were given without any documents of transfer, but in the presence of witnesses. Such oral contracts were literally "bespoken," *i.e.,* BEQUEATHED. This ancient word has been preserved only because of the traditional jargon still used in wills and other legal documents.

The contraction WON'T is another verbal relic, and stood for the older "woll not," for "will not." German still retains the two forms. The utter confusion existing between "I had" and "I would" has arisen from the use of the contraction "I'd," which is substituted for both forms. But despite the insistence of most purists upon "I would rather," the idiom "I HAD rather" is not only correct, but has been in use for hundreds of years. This construction is a petrified example of the old past subjunctive, still used in German, and which we also employ when we say "If I WERE king," instead of "If I was king."

When we say "He sleeps DAYS and works NIGHTS, but he does not work SUNDAYS," or "He goes to Florida WINTERS and lives in Vermont SUMMERS," most of us think of these forms as plurals. Actually, however, they are old adverbial genitives, and the final *s* is the same as that in "the dog's tail." The same construction appears in NOWADAYS, SIDEWAYS, and in the idiom "I NEEDS must go," as well as in the words ONCE, TWICE, THRICE, HENCE, and THENCE, which used to be *ones, twies, thries, hennes,* and *thennes.* While on the subject of adverbs, we may go to the aid of sign painters and legitimize "Go SLOW." This adverb, along with FAST, QUICK, CHEAP, SOUND, HIGH, LOW, and STILL, belongs to an old group of adverbs which once ended in *-e* instead of *-ly*. The adverbial ending has simply disappeared. The word never was "slowly"! And we should never think of saying "fastly."

Do you know that we have an adverbial THE in common use, as well as the definite article? An analysis of the sentence "THE sooner you do it, THE better it will be" makes it obvious that this THE cannot possibly be a definite article, but the fact is not generally realized. The meaning of the above sentence is "*By however much* sooner you do it, *by so much* will it be better." In Anglo-Saxon the article was spelled *the,* as it is today, but the adverb was once *thy.* And here we may as well slay the legend that has given rise to "YE Olde Coffee Shoppe." In the days when all books were written by hand, scribes tried to simplify matters by using one symbol for a group of letters. Both þ and ꝩ were used for *th,* and when manuscripts were hurriedly written these symbols often looked like *y*. Later readers of these manuscripts then mistook the symbols for *y* and assumed that "the" was once YE.

Now that we are back on the subject of words that have come about through misunderstandings, we find many others that have been radically altered through a wrong division of syllables. Today we should not recognize "nadder," "nap-ron," and "nauger," if we saw these words in print, but they were once what we now know as ADDER, APRON, and AUGER. People used to say "a nadder," "a napron," "a nauger," but gradually the words came to be thought of as "an ADDER," "an APRON," and "an AUGER." In the same way, AUGHT (zero) came from "naught," and we now have both forms. ORANGE was once "norange," but this change occurred in French before we borrowed the word. UMPIRE is another example of the same error. The earlier form is "ompere" and this came by wrong division from "a nompere." The latter form is the Old French *nomper*, meaning "not equal," "uneven" (compare "peer" — our law provides that we shall be tried before a jury of our "peers," our "equals"). The sense, then, of *nomper* or UMPIRE is that of an "odd man," a third party called in to settle a dispute. Perhaps the most spectacular example of this class of words is the term HUMBLE PIE. It seems almost like sacrilege, but "to eat HUMBLE PIE" has properly not the slightest connection with the word "humble." The phrase was once (an) "umble" pie, and this was formed by wrong division of (a) "numble" pie. "Numbles," from Old French *nombles*, meant "entrails," and the pie was made for the servants' table from the heart, liver, etc.

In the cases of NOTCH and NICKNAME exactly the opposite has taken place. The *n* of "an" has been carried over to the following word. The original forms were "otch" and "ekename," a name that was "added" to another. This "eke" is the same word we find in the phrase "to eke out a living."

The same confusion has arisen in French, but here the

definite article has been the worst offender. This is due largely to the French use of *l'* for either *le* or *la* (all three forms meaning "the"). Thus JADE is from the French *le jade*, the jade, but the French form was once *l'ejade*. The French had a terrible time trying to decide what the word OMELET was to be. This culinary delicacy started out from the Latin word *lamella*, a thin plate, which gave a French form *lamelle*. With the definite article before it, the result was *la lamelle*, the omelet, and this by wrong division gave *l'alemelle*. But we are still a long way from OMELET! *Alemelle* was first corrupted to *alemette*, and then the *m* and *l* changed places, giving *amelette*, which later became *omelette*.

The word AMMUNITION is less imposing, but it too has come about through wrong division. The original French form was *la munition*, and then erroneously, *l'ammunition*. We now have both forms. LARIAT is our own corruption of the Spanish *la reata*, the lasso. We have done the same thing to the Spanish *el lagarto*, the lizard, and the result is ALLIGATOR.

The French examples mentioned above bring to mind another curious example of a French corruption. Of anyone who mangles their language, the French say: "Il parle français COMME UNE VACHE ESPAGNOLE." ("He speaks French LIKE A SPANISH COW.") the original form of the phrase, while not so colorful, was somewhat more enlightening, for the expression was once "Il parle français *comme un Basque, l'espagnol*," which, translated, reads: "He speaks French *as a Basque* (speaks) *Spanish*" (*i.e.*, very badly).

In the case of LARIAT and ALLIGATOR we have made the article a part of the word. The same thing has happened to some words derived from Arabic, most of them through Spanish. The Arabic article *al* was falsely considered a part of the word and so was added to it (see ARTICHOKE, page 24). In this manner we have AL-FALFA, AL-KALI, AL-GEBRA, and even ADMIR-AL. The latter is really the word "Emir" and came to us through the French *amiral*, but the Arabic form was *amir al* (*bahr*), ruler of the (sea). LUTE is the result of a similar error. The Arabic original was *al'ud,* the lute.

This phenomenon of wrong division has occurred, however, in still other circumstances. The diminutive ending -LET, for example, was originally the French ending -*et,* and came about through wrong division of French nouns ending in -*l.* HAMLET is the Old French *hamel* (now *hameau*), village, plus the diminutive -*et.* In such words the ending came to be thought of as -LET, so we now have words like STARLET, STREAMLET, etc. This reminds me of the tale of the city cousin, vacationing on the farm, who came out one morning and exclaimed: "Oooh, see the pretty little cowlets!" To which the farmer replied: "Them ain't cowlets, Ruthie, them's bullets!"

TAWDRY was once used particularly in the phrase "TAWDRY lace," and referred to a cheap ornate lace sold at "St. Audry's" Fair in England. Our Canadian friends have election districts which they call RIDINGS. The word used to be "thriding" and in England meant a "third" part of a shire. In a phrase such as "north thriding," the two words were run together, and they then became "north RIDING."

Singular and plural forms have sometimes been confused. PEA is from an older "pease" and goes back to the Greek *pison,* pea. "Pease" came to be regarded as a plural and so the new singular was formed. The same phenomenon has occurred in the words CHERRY, for the earlier "cherris," from the Old Norman French form *cherise,* and SHERRY, for "sherris," from the Spanish (*vino de*) *Xeres,* (wine of) Jerez. The "one-hoss SHAY" was an erroneous singular formed from the French *chaise,* which came to be looked upon as a plural. Both forms are used in consecutive lines of the poem:

> It was on the terrible Earthquake-day
> That the deacon finished the one-hoss shay.

> Now in the building of chaises, I tell you what,
> There is always *somewhere* a weakest spot . . .

The "heathen CHINEE" is another example of this same confusion. In like manner, a theatre MARQUEE was once a "marquees," an English version of the French *marquise*. (A MARQUEE was erected to shelter a noble lady, a *marquise*.) RICHES is now a plural noun, but was once singular, from the French *richesse*, wealth. In the case of TRUCE, the opposite has happened. This word was once "trewes," the plural of "trewe," a compact or promise. I suppose the word came to be used in the plural because a TRUCE is usually the result of several "trewes." When "trewes" finally acquired its present meaning, it was soon looked upon as a singular noun, and the spelling was altered to make it look like a singular form.

I have recently observed an example of this same process of wrong division. About ten years ago a Mr. Waite moved into the vicinity of my summer home, and in these ten years his name has definitely changed to "Waites," as far as his neighbors are concerned. They first formed the erroneous plural "Waiteses" when referring to the family, and now everyone says "Mr. Waites."

Chapter III

SISTERS AND COUSINS,
RECKONED UP IN DOZENS

WOULD you ever associate a pair of antlers with a binocular? or an apron with a mop? or a ship's binnacle with the word "habitation"? And can you imagine why a canary was named for a dog? or what the carnage of war has to do with a carnival? or why the word "conscience" has "science" as one part of it?

Someone has estimated that from approximately 150 Latin and Greek roots, we have derived some 13,000 words of our English vocabulary. This is one reason why the English language is capable of expressing more shades of meaning than any other language in the world. Many of these words, however, have been so altered both in form and sense that we do not often associate them, either with their primitive ancestors, or, in the case of words of common origin, with each other. Words that we have borrowed from Latin and Greek in fairly recent times are the easiest to recognize, for they are quite similar to their ancient originals. On the other hand, those which literally "grew" out of Latin into French, and were borrowed by us from French, and those that were introduced into English in the earliest times, have been so changed as to defy recognition.

Sometimes, as with ANTLER-BINOCULAR, APRON-MOP, and BINNACLE-HABITATION, words of common origin now have absolutely no resemblance to each other. The first pair comes from the Latin word for "eye": *oculus.* An OCULIST is an "eye doctor." BINOCULAR is obvious enough then if we remember that the prefix *bi-* means "two." Through BINOCULARS we can see with "two eyes" at the same time. The relationship of ANTLER to *oculus* is not so apparent. This word came to us through the Old French form *antoillier* [ANT(oil)L(i)ER], which went back to a Popular Latin phrase *antocularem* (*ramum*), "(a branch) in front of the eyes." *Antocularem* is a compound of *ante*, in front of, and *oculus.* But *oculus* had a secondary meaning of "bud" (the sense is the same as when we speak of the "eye" of a potato), and from this idea was formed the Latin verb *inoculare*, to implant, which gives us INOCULATE. Another less obvious derivation from *oculus* is the verb to INVEIGLE. This word came to us through the Old Norman French form *enveogler,* which corresponded to the Central French *aveugler,* to blind, from Latin *ab*, from, and *oculus.* Originally INVEIGLE meant "to blindfold" or "to hood-wink," and so developed the meaning of "to lure by deception."

APRON and MOP are both from the Latin *mappa*, cloth, napkin. Already we see a connection, as far as the sense is concerned. MOP is just another form of the word MAP (early maps were painted on cloth), and the relationship of these two words to *mappa* is clear. As we saw in the last chapter, APRON was once "a napron," and this is the Old French *naperon,* tablecloth (literally, "a big napkin," just as "balloon" is "a big ball"), which came from *mappa.* (The shift from *m* to *n* is common.) The modern French "tablecloth" is *nappe,* and our NAPKIN is this word with the diminutive ending added.

A BINNACLE is a "housing" for a ship's compass. This word is a corruption of "bittacle," from the Spanish *bitacula,* which meant first "abode" and later "binnacle." The Spanish word came from the Latin *habitaculum,* a little dwelling, which in turn is from the Latin verb *habitare,* to dwell. From this verb we also get HABITATION.

The PILGRIM fathers had to live largely by AGRICULTURE, but we do not immediately see any relationship between these two words. Both, however, go back ultimately to the Latin *ager,* field. AGRICULTURE is "the culture of the fields," and its derivation is quite simple. The word PILGRIM, on the other hand, is not so obvious. We find the older forms "pilegrim" and "pelegrim," which came to us through Old French from a Latin *peregrinus.* This Latin word meant "stranger," and in turn was formed from *pereger,* "one going abroad." *Pereger* is simply a compound of *per,* through, and *ager,* field, and meant literally "one going through the fields."

There are other words whose relationship is still clearly indicated by their spelling, but whose meanings have wandered far apart. CANARY and CANINE are both from the Latin *canis,* dog. CANARIES came from the Canary Islands, which were named *Canaria* because of the large dogs brought there by the Romans. Both CARNAGE and CARNIVAL go back to Italian words, formed ultimately from the Latin *carnem,* meat, flesh. (CARNAL sins are "sins of the flesh"). CARNAGE is from the Italian *carnaggio,* slaughter, while CARNIVAL is the Italian *carnevale,* Shrove Tuesday. The Italian word came from the

Latin phrase *carnem levare,* to put away (*i.e.,* stop eating) meat. *Carnem levare* first became *carnem levale,* through a shift from *r* to *l,* and then the two words were run together: *carne(mle)vale.* CONSCIENCE and SCIENCE are both from the Latin *scientia,* knowledge. Your CONSCIENCE tells you "you should *know* better," and SCIENCE really means "knowledge." The verb to INVESTIGATE and the noun VESTIGE seem rather far apart in meaning, but their relationship becomes more obvious when we realize that to INVESTIGATE means "to trace," while a VESTIGE is "a trace." Both words are derived from the Latin *vestigium,* footprint, trace.

Now let's take *caput,* the Latin word for "head," and see what a varied assortment of words we have gotten from it. Those which have come directly from the Latin contain the letters *cap, cep,* or *cip:* DECAPITATE, to take the "head" off; CAPTAIN, the "headman"; CAPITULATE, which first meant to arrange in "headings" or CHAPTERS (the *ch* for *c* is a French variation), hence, to draw up an agreement under various "headings," and finally, "to surrender" according to the terms agreed upon. CAPTION would seem to belong here but, as we shall see shortly, this is quite a different word. Then we have BICEPS, a muscle with two "heads" or places of attachment; CAPE, a "headland"; PRECIPICE, first, a falling "head-long," and then a steep place where one is liable to take such a fall; and CABBAGE, which came to us indirectly through the French word *caboche,* a slang term for "head."

As we have seen in the case of the word CHAPTER, the *c* of *caput* normally became *ch* in French, and so we have CHIEF and CHIEFTAIN, a "headman." These two words are from *chief,* the Old French word for "head," which remains in modern French only as CHEF, the "headman" in the kitchen. The French now use *tête* for "head" and we have borrowed this word in the phrase TÊTE-A-TÊTE. *Tête* comes from Popular Latin slang. The Romans called the head a "pot" (*testa*), just as we refer to it as a "bean." Other words from the Old

French *chief* are ACHIEVE, "to get *ahead*," from the Old French
phrase *venir à chief,* literally "to come to the head" of some-
thing, MISCHIEF, the "bad head" to which things come, and
KERCHIEF, from the Old French *covrechief,* "cover-head." A
HANDKERCHIEF is literally a "hand-cover-head," and a POCKET
HANDKERCHIEF. . . . !

The words CATTLE and CHATTEL are less obvious derivations
from *caput.* We get CATTLE from Norman French, where the *c*
did not become *ch,* while CHATTEL is the old Parisian French
form of the same word. The idea behind both words was
"chief" property. When we say that a man owns so many
"head" of cattle, we do not refer to their heads any more than
to their tails. In ancient times "cattle" was generally synonymous with "property" and even with "money." Roman taxes
were collected according to the number of cattle a man
owned. PECUNIARY is from the Latin word *pecunia,* money,
and to PECULATE is to embezzle. Both words go back to the
Latin *pecu,* cattle. Even PECULIAR is from the same root, and
was formed on the Latin noun *peculium,* private property.
Similarly, our word FEE first meant "cattle" and then "money"
(German *Vieh,* cattle, is the same word and is even pronounced "fee"). A FELLOW was originally "one who lays down
a (partnership) FEE." The Anglo-Saxon form was *feolaga,*
composed of *feoh,* cattle, property, fee, and *laga,* a laying
down. (Compare the German *Verlag,* the first meaning of
which is the CAPITAL necessary to an undertaking.)

The word CAPTION was mentioned above as not being
derived from *caput,* even though it has come to mean "heading." CAPTION is rather the Latin *captionem,* a seizing, from
the verb *capere,* to seize, to take. The original meaning of
CAPTION was the "seizure" of a defendant in a law-suit, and
the word still has this sense in England. It then came to mean
the "heading" of a legal document setting forth the parties
to an action, and now refers to any heading or title, especially
to the title of an illustration. The relationship to *capere* is more

apparent in CAPTURE, to "seize," and CAPTIVE, one who has been "seized." A CAPTIOUS person is one too ready to "take" offense. If you CHASE a person, you try to CATCH him, and both these words go back to *capere*. CHASE has come through the Old French *chacier* (now *chasser*, to chase, hunt), and CATCH is the Old Norman French form of the same word (*cachier*). These two words are properly from the Latin *captare*, but this in turn was formed from *capere* and had about the same meaning. Even CABLE is an Old French word coming from a Popular Latin *capulum*, a rope, something to "take" hold of.

One would never associate FOREIGN, FOREST, and FORFEIT unless he knew the key meaning of the first syllable of these words, the Latin *foris*, outside. Anything that is FOREIGN to us is "outside" our immediate knowledge or surroundings. FOREST derives from the Popular Latin pharse (*silva*) *forestis*, (a wood) "outside" (the walls). We do have the adjective "silvan" in English which means "pertaining to a forest," but for the noun we have adopted (through French) the second half of this Latin phrase, and the word FOREST has really nothing to do with a "woods." The verb to FORFEIT once meant to do something "outside" the law, and a FORFEIT was the consequence of such transgression.

The relationship between DISK and DISCUS is clear enough. Both go back to the Greek word *diskos*, a disk. But have you ever connected these words with DISH, DESK, and DAIS? DISH was borrowed from the Latin form *discus* way back in Anglo-Saxon times, and has become thoroughly naturalized. *Discus* finally came to mean "table" in Latin and in Late Latin times the word *desca*, DESK, was formed from it. The meaning of DAIS is analogous and this word was borrowed from the Old French *deis*.

CAPER and CAPRICE are somewhat related in thought, but what about CABRIOLET? CAPER is simply the Latin word for "goat," while CAPRICE is from the Italian *capriccio*, a sudden start, like the leap of a "goat." A CABRIOLET is really a "puddle

jumper," and was originally a very light two-wheeled carriage.
The word comes from the French *cabriole,* a goat's leap, again
from the Italian *capriola,* a little goat. We have a word CAPRI-
OLE in English, used to describe a leap made by a horse on all
fours without advancing.

The capers of a goat bring to mind another series of words
derived from the Latin verb *salire* and its related *saltare,* both
meaning "to jump." A SALIENT fact is an outstanding one, one
that "jumps" out at you. A rubber band is RESILIENT because it
will "jump" back into place when stretched. A SALLY is a
sudden rushing out or "leaping" forward of troops. EXILE is
from the Latin *exsilium,* banishment, formed from *ex-,* out,
and *salire,* the idea being that of "getting out in a hurry."
RESULT is from the Latin *resultare* (*re-* plus *saltare*), to re-
bound. EXULT is similarly formed and means "to leap for joy,"
while if you INSULT a man, you literally "jump on him."
DESULTORY is from the Latin *desultor,* a circus rider, and means
"jumping" aimlessly from one thing to another.

How would you associate a BRACE of ducks or a BRACE of
pistols with a BRACELET and a PRETZEL? BRACE comes from the
Old French *brase* or *brache,* meaning "two arms" (from the
Latin plural noun *brachia,* arms), and has kept the idea of
"two" as well as that of "arm." A BRACE of pistols is a "pair,"
but the idea of "arm" remains when we use BRACE to mean a
"support." BRACELET goes back to a Late Latin word *bracellus,*
an "arm" band, while PRETZEL is a German word that had
an earlier form *bretzel.* This word too is apparently derived
from *bracellus.* EMBRACE belongs to the same family. Its
relationship is plain.

The Latin verb *tangere,* to touch, and its past participle
tactus, touched, have given us quite a variety of words. If
a thing is TANGIBLE, it is real or capable of being "touched."
A TANGENT line in geometry is a line "touching" another line
or surface, and CONTIGUOUS (*-tig-* is a stem from *tangere*)
likewise means "touching" or adjoining. Then from *tactus*

we get the adjective TACTILE, pertaining to the sense of "touch," and the noun TACT, which means first the "sense of touch," then any keen faculty of perception, likened to the sense of touch, and finally a delicate sense of what is "fitting and proper." Anything that is INTACT is "untouched," while if we come into CONTACT with something, we "touch" it, and we try to avoid CONTACT with a CONTAGIOUS disease.

From *tangere* the Romans formed another verb, *taxare*, which also meant "to touch," but with the added sense of "to feel" or "to handle." From this word came the Old French *taster*, to touch or to TASTE (the form in modern French is *tâter*). From the idea of "handling," the Latin *taxare* came to mean "to appraise" or "to rate," and so our TAXES are based on an "appraisal" of our property, our income, etc. Sometimes TAXES were assessed as a definite amount of labor in lieu of money, and hence we have the word TASK. This word came about from a transposition of the letters *s* and *c*. From the noun *taxa* (which was really *tacsa*) there arose in Late Latin times the variant *tasca*. This latter word gave the two Old French forms *tasque*, now spelled TASK in English, and *tasche*, which has remained in modern French as *tâche*, a TASK.

The dread disease CANCER and the CHANCELLOR of the Exchequer both go back to *cancer*, the Latin word for "crab." The sores produced by CANCER were supposed to resemble the claws of a crab, and CANKER derives from the same idea. CHANCELLOR was once the lowly Roman *cancellarius*, an usher in a law court. This word came from *cancelli*, the "crab-like" latticed railings around the judgment seat in courts of the Late Roman Empire; a church CHANCEL is separated from the nave by a similar latticework. CANCEL is from the Old French *canceller*, to draw lines across like a latticework.

An AMBULATORY patient in a hospital is one who is able to "walk" and is not confined to bed. This word comes from the Latin *ambulare*, to walk. AMBLE goes back to the same word, but through French. Similarly, AMBULANCE stems from the French phrase (*hôpital*) *ambulant*, "walking (hospital)."

How would you associate a "pebble" with CALCULUS, the branch of higher mathematics? This is the Latin *calculus*, a pebble, and we also have in English an adjective CALCULOUS that means "gritty." Primitive peoples often used pebbles for counting or CALCULATING, hence the relationship between these words. The early inhabitants of Mexico used pebbles for counting, and in their language 1-2-3 was "one-stone," "two-stones," "three-stones." We do not speak of a SCRUPLE in our shoe, but this is the Latin *scrupulus*, a very small pebble, especially a sharp one, whence the idea of "uneasiness," "doubt," and "scruple." A SCRUPLE is also a very small apothecary's weight, and this use of the word dates from Roman times.

We have a number of words which derive from the idea of "flowing." As we have seen (page 31), ABOUND is from the Latin verb *undare*, to overflow, which also gives us the adjective ABUNDANT. AFFLUENT means "having an abundance" and comes from *fluere*, to flow. A FLUENT speaker is one whose words "flow" easily, and a FLUID is anything that "flows." FLUORESCENT contains the idea of "flowing" rays. FLUX means the "flow" of the tide or it may be a substance used to promote the melting or "flowing" of metals. This word is from *fluxus*, the past participle of *fluere*. There was also an older past participle *fluctus*, and from this we have FLUCTUATE, to rise and fall (the way a wave "flows"). FLUME is from the Latin *flumen*, a river, which also comes from *fluere*. The much disputed city of Fiume is the Italian form of the same word. Then the Romans had the word *fundere*, to pour. From this we have FUNNEL, and from the past participle *fusus*, poured, we get FUSE. To FUSE is to "melt," and a FUSE is placed in an electric circuit because it will "melt" or blow out before anything else. REFUND is from the Latin compound *re-fundere*, which meant "to pour back," or, when used of solid objects, "to throw back."

The latter meaning gives REFUSE. If you REFUSE something, you "throw it back," while the noun REFUSE means anything that is "thrown away" as worthless. To REJECT also means "to refuse" and is from the Latin *jactare*, to throw. Just as REJECT means "to throw back," so INJECT means "to throw in," and OBJECT, "to throw toward." Through French we get JET, through which a stream of liquid or gas is "thrown," JETTY, a pier "thrown" out over the water, JETTISON, to "throw" overboard, and JETSAM, goods "thrown" overboard.

We do not think of a PROMENADE as being very MENACING, but it once was, at least for cattle. MENACE is from the Latin *minaciae*, threats, and from this noun was formed the verb *minari*, to threaten. PROMENADE is from the Late Latin *prominare*, to drive (beasts) ahead "by threatening." The idea of a walk was once incidental.

A JOURNAL and a DIARY are essentially the same thing (both are "day books," while JOURNAL may also mean a "daily" paper), but the two words do not in the least resemble each other. The word DIURNAL serves as a connecting link to bring them closer together. DIURNAL means "pertaining to the day," as opposed to "nocturnal." This is the Latin *diurnalis*, daily, which is likewise the source of the French *journal*. (If you are wondering how this *di-* became *j-*, consider what happens to our own "did you" when we make "di-jou" or even "di-ja" out of it.) Other related words which we have borrowed from French are: ADJOURN, to put off until another "day," SOJOURN, to stay, to spend a "day," and JOURNEY, once "a day's march." The Latin adjective *diurnalis* was formed from the noun *dies*, day, which also gave rise to the word *diaria*. This latter word had especial reference to "daily pay," but is the source of the English DIARY.

A man would not care to use an ABRASIVE on his face to take off his whiskers, but this word comes from the same root as RAZOR. They are both from *rasus*, the past participle of the Latin verb *radere*, which had all the meanings of the various words we have derived from it. This verb meant "to scratch," the idea retained in ABRASIVE; "to scratch out," to ERASE; "to strip," "to lay waste," to RAZE; and "to shave" — the French word is *raser*, and from it we get RAZOR.

The Latin *albus*, white, has given us such varied words as ALBINO, which we borrowed from the Portuguese (who first applied the word to white Negroes), ALBUMEN, the "white" of an egg, AUBURN (for "alburn"), which once meant "whitish," and DAUB, originally meaning to "whitewash." Even the poetic word ALBION for "England" comes from "the white cliffs of Dover."

DOCILE, DOCTOR, and DOCUMENT all stem from the Latin verb *docere*, to teach. A DOCILE animal or child is one easily "taught" or managed. DOCTOR used to mean "teacher," and the original sense of DOCUMENT was "lesson."

Latin had the verb *trahere*, to draw, and also a derived form *tractare*, to draw, handle, or manage. From these we have a large family of words in English. A TRACTABLE individual is one easily managed or "drawn" along. A metal is TRACTILE if it can be "drawn out" or lengthened. A TRACTOR is a TRACTION vehicle which "draws" a load. A TRACT of land is a "stretch," the extent to which that particular area is "drawn out." Then of course we have the compounds: ATTRACT, to draw to, CONTRACT, to draw together, DETRACT, to draw away from, RETRACT, to draw back, or to withdraw, etc. RETREAT also means "to draw back," and this word introduces another group from the same source which has come to us through the medium of French. When we speak of a personal TRAIT, we refer to some touch or "drawing" of a character. This idea comes out more clearly in the compound PORTRAIT. To TRAIL anything is to "draw" it, a TRAIN is "drawn" by a locomotive, and when we TRACE a picture, we "draw" lines. TREAT and TREATY take us back to the meaning of "handle." You TREAT a person well if you "handle" him well, and a TREATY is made between nations only after "handling" matters in dispute.

The words TREK, TRACK, and TRIGGER also have the idea of "drawing" or "pulling" and have come to us from the Dutch word *treccan,* to pull; while a money TILL ("drawer") and the TILLER of a boat are from the Anglo-Saxon word *tillen,* to draw. To TILL the soil, however, does not come from the idea of "drawing" a plow, but is from an old word meaning "to strive."

CHAPERON and CHAPEL have rather different connotations, but they are both from the Latin word *cappa,* cloak. CHAPERON was originally a "hooded cloak," then the word was transferred to the "hood" itself, and finally to an older woman, the wearer of the hood. CHAPEL is thought to have come from the fact that St. Martin's "cloak" was preserved in a shrine in France, which came to be known as a *chapelle.* The cloak's custodian then became the CHAPLAIN. CAPE has essentially the same meaning as *cappa,* while CAP (like the French *chapeau*) refers again to the "hood" of the cloak. With this background, the word ESCAPE takes on a picturesque meaning, for the sense is that of slipping "out of one's cloak" and thus making a getaway.

This word CLOAK came to have its present meaning only by analogy, for it is the Old Norman French *cloke,* bell (compare modern French *cloche* and German *Glocke*). The modern sense of CLOAK arose from a "bell-shaped" cape. CLOCK is the same word, and this meaning is presumably due to the fact that the hours were sounded on "bells" and that CLOCKS were erected in "bell" towers. Another word for "cloak," MANTLE, from the Old French *mantel* (now *manteau*) and Latin *mantellum,* cloak, has its counterpart in MANTEL, a "cloak" to hide the rough masonry of a fireplace. The two forms are only different spellings of the same word.

We might appropriately make CHOWDER in a CHAFING dish, for both words are derivatives of the Latin *calidus,* hot. *Calidus* has given the French *chaud,* hot, and *chauffer,* to heat. So a CHAFING dish is only a "heating" dish. We now use CHAFE with the sense of "to rub," but friction generates "heat." CHOWDER is from the French *chaudière,* a pot for "heating" food. CHAUFFEUR is the French word for "stoker." Finally, we have CAULDRON, from the Norman French *caudron,* a big pot.

BULLET means "little ball" and is an Old French diminutive of the Latin *bulla,* ball (*bulla* first meant "bubble," and came from the verb *bullire,* to boil). A Papal BULL referred originally to the leaden "ball-shaped" seal on the document, then to the document itself. From this sense of "edict" is derived the word BULLETIN, from the Italian *bulletino,* a little edict, a notice.

"A STITCH in time saves nine," but what has this to do with Emily Post's ETIQUETTE? These and many other words take us back to an old Indo-European root *stig,* with the basic meaning of "prick." In words from Germanic sources the form is *stik.* Hence to STICK is to "prick" or "puncture," and STITCH has the same sense. Both words are from the Anglo-Saxon *stician,* to prick. STICK has also developed a meaning of "adhesion" or STICKINESS. From meaning "to prick" or "to thrust into," the word took on the sense of "to remain imbedded," and finally that of "to adhere." Thus we have STICKER, an adhesive label. The French word *étiquette* comes from a Germanic source, and it too has developed the meaning of "label." The word also means TICKET, however, and is the source of this English word. (The French have borrowed the word back from English, and now use *ticket* for railroad and bus tickets.) Our modern use of ETIQUETTE derives from the custom, which once prevailed at the French Court, of posting on the walls prescribed rules of conduct. These posters or STICKERS were *étiquettes,* and the sense was then transferred from the posters to the rules themselves. Finally, we have the word STOCKADE, a space enclosed by pointed "stakes" or "sticks." This word also is ultimately from German, but came to us through French and Spanish. The Spanish form was *estacada,* from *estaca,* a pointed stake. The French changed it to *estocade,* from which the English is derived.

We find the same root, in the form *stig*, in Greek and Latin. The word STIGMA is a Greek term meaning a "prick." A STIGMA was a brand burnt on slaves, just as we brand cattle. The same root turns up again in INSTIGATE and STIMULATE (for "sti(g)mulate"), both of which contain the notion of "pricking" or "prodding." INSTINCT is a related word, and meant first "instigation," then "suggestion," then "impulse," and finally, "a natural impulse." Similarly, STYLUS goes back to the Greek *stulos*, a pointed instrument used by the ancients for "pricking" or writing on wax tablets. The Latin form *stilus* came to mean "a setting down in writing," and then, "a manner or STYLE of writing." The word STILETTO is an Italian diminutive of *stilus*.

The famous definition of "latticework" in Samuel Johnson's Dictionary was "something reticulated or DECUSSATED, with interstices between the intersections" (!). Any relationship between DECUSSATE, which means "to divide," and the DEAN of a college would seem rather obscure. Both are from the Latin *decem*, ten, which has also given us DECIMAL, pertaining to the number "ten," DECEMBER, in Roman times the "tenth" month, and DECIMATE, literally "to kill every *tenth* man." DEAN is from the Latin *decanus*, which originally meant "someone in charge of *ten* others." DECUSSATE first meant "to mark with an X" (the sign for "ten"), and so came to have the sense of "to intersect," "to cut," or "to divide."

INTERSECT brings us to the Latin *secare*, to cut or divide. This word gives us the obvious SECTION and SECTOR, as well as INSECT, a "divided" or "notched" bug. Interestingly enough, the words SCORE and TALLY also contain the idea of "notch," for notching a stick was once the method of "keeping score." SCORE is from an old word meaning "notch," while TALLY comes from the French *tailler*, to cut, from which we likewise get TAILOR.

The words CAR, CARRIAGE, and CHARIOT are obviously related, but what about CARICATURE? These all go back to the

Latin *carrus,* cart. A CARPENTER was originally a "wagon maker," and CAREER comes through the French *carrière,* race course, from the Latin *carraria* (*via*), carriage (road). CARICATURE, as well as CHARGE and CARGO, comes from the notion of "loading" a cart. A CARGO is a "load" and the idea of "loading" is implied when we CHARGE a gun or a storage battery. CARICATURE is from the Italian *carricatura,* a "loading" or exaggeration.

From the Latin *plumbus,* lead, we get PLUMBER, one who works in "lead," tin, zinc, etc. A PLUMMET or PLUMB bob is a weight, often a piece of "lead," attached to a string, used to determine perpendicularity. We say that a bird shot in mid-air PLUMMETS or PLUNGES to the ground. PLUNGE is from the French *plonger,* to dive, and derives from an earlier *plomber,* to sound the depth of water (with a lead PLUMMET). The French APLOMB, which we have adopted, means first "perpendicularity," then "equilibrium," and hence "self-assurance."

From this same idea of weight we get such different words as POUND and PENSIVE. These go back to the Latin *pendere,* to weigh, related to the verb *pendere,* to hang. To PONDER is to think or "weigh in the mind," and the adjective PONDEROUS means "heavy." The French *penser,* to think, is similarly derived from the sense of "to weigh in the mind," and gives us PENSIVE. Coins were once "weighed" instead of minted, and so we get PENSION, literally "a weighing out" of money. SPEND also means "to weigh out" and is from the compound *expendere.* This word was borrowed very early, from the missionaries whom St. Augustine sent to England. The Latin word for "pound" was *libra,* which first meant a "level" and then the "beam" of a scale. *Libra* is the source of the French *livre,* pound, and the Italian *lira,* a unit of money, as well as of the British symbol £, for the "pound" sterling, and the abbreviation *lb.* for "pound." The word POUND itself, on the other hand, is from the Latin phrase (*libra*) *pondo,* (a pound) "in weight." To EXAMINE has the same sense of "weighing in the mind" as to PONDER. In Roman times an *examen* was the "needle" on a set of balances. The Latin *examinare* had both the meaning of "to weigh" and that of "to ponder" or "to examine." DELIBERATE came about in a similar manner, for this word is formed from the Latin prefix *de-* and *librare,* to weigh.

From the Old French *grape,* a vine hook, we have both GRAPE and GRAPPLE. From the original meaning of "vine hook" (the idea of "hook" is retained in GRAPPLE), *grape* came to mean "a bunch of grapes." In French this word (now spelled *grappe*) still means "a cluster of grapes," but we use the word for a single grape. In the same way, RAISIN once meant "a bunch of grapes."

Do you see any connection between the CANONS of the Church, a military CANNON, the Grand CANYON, and a kitchen CANISTER? These are all from the Latin *canna,* a reed, which in turn was borrowed from Greek. Our most obviously related word is sugar CANE, but the word CANE in all its meanings is from this source. The Greek *kanna* gave another Greek word *kanon,* which was first a "reed" used as a measuring rule. Then, as has happened with our own "rule," the sense was carried over to "regulation," from which arises the ecclesiastical use of CANON. A "reed" is a small "tube," while a CANNON is fundamentally nothing but a large "tube." In the same way, CANYON is the Spanish word for "tube." CANISTER goes back to the Greek *kanastron,* a wicker basket, a basket made of "reeds."

The words LINEN, LINGERIE, and LINSEED can readily be associated with the Latin *linum,* flax, but LINING, LINE and LINEAGE are from the same root. We now speak of a LINING to a coat simply because LININGS were once made of LINEN. LINE and LINEAGE, on the other hand, are from the Latin *linea,* which first meant "a string made of *flax,*" and then any kind of a "string" or LINE.

We all shed tears for the DAMSEL in distress, especially if she is in a deep, dark DUNGEON under the DOMINATION of a tyrant. These and other words are from the Latin *dominus* and *domina*, "lord" and "lady." DAMSEL is the French *damoiselle*, a diminutive of *dame*, lady (from *domina*). Similarly, the Spanish DON (Juan) is a derivation from the masculine form *dominus*, which survives in English only in the phrase "DAN Cupid." DOMINATE stems from the Latin *dominare*, to rule, to "lord it" over others. DOMINION is the Latin *dominium*, right of "lordship." DUNGEON is from the Old French *donjon*, derived from a Late Latin *domnionem*, a DOMINATING tower of a castle, under which were vaults used as prisons.

These examples of word families, which have by no means exhausted the possibilities, have been derived almost exclusively from Greek and Latin roots. As a nightcap, let's have a look at an Anglo-Saxon family that may surprise you. The three words THRILL, NOSTRIL, and THOROUGH all go back to THROUGH in the first instance. THOROUGH is only another form of THROUGH (if we cook anything THOROUGHLY, we cook it "THROUGH and THROUGH"). THRILL had an earlier form "thirl," which came from Anglo-Saxon *thyrlian*, to pierce "through." *Thyrlian* was formed from the noun *thyrel*, hole, which in turn went back to *thurh*, the original form of THROUGH. If you are THRILLED with joy, you are literally "pierced" with it, and a NOSTRIL is simply a "nose-hole," or, in Anglo-Saxon, a *nosthyrl*.

Chapter IV

AND THEREBY HANGS A TALE

SOME words have interesting historical associations in connection with their development, or derive from ancient customs and beliefs, long since forgotten. The stories behind these words not only throw light on their meaning, but make them more vivid and interesting to us today.

CULPRIT is such a word, and its formation was really an accident. The expression dates from the times when Anglo-French was used in the law courts of England. The original form was *culpable: prest*, and the meaning: (the defendant is) "guilty" (and we are) "ready" (to prove it). In official records the phrase was abbreviated to *cul.prest*, later corrupted to *cul.prit*. Eventually, the clerks of the courts came to use the abbreviated form orally, instead of the original formula *culpable: prest*, in some such manner as: "*Cul.prit*. How will you be tried?" Used in this way, the original sense was finally forgotten, and CULPRIT was taken to mean the prisoner.

The EXCHEQUER in England is now the Treasury, but it was formerly a court of law, established to recover unpaid taxes. In such a court a "checkered" cloth covered the table on which the amounts due were figured up. The word comes through the Old French *eschequier*, chess-board, and goes back ultimately to the Persian *shah*, king.

CHEAT points a finger at early grafters in Britain. The word is a shortened form of "escheat" which came through Old French from Latin *ex-cadere*, to fall. An "escheater" was an officer of the Crown who attended to the "escheats," lands which might revert or "fall" to the king in default of heirs. Due to the natural hazards of the profession, the term came to imply "a dishonest escheater" and then was applied to any kind of CHEATER.

BANAL takes us back to feudal times, when serfs were obliged to have their grain ground at the mill of their lord, thus increasing his revenues. These mills were called "bannal mills" because they had to be used as ordered by the *bannum* or proclamation of the master. This *bannum* is a Late Latin word which came from German, and is also the source of our BANNS of marriage. In the XVIth century "bannal" had come to mean simply "common to all," but the word has since deteriorated into "commonplace" or "trite." The verbs BAN and

BANISH are from the same source. A thing was BANNED or a person BANISHED by an "order" or "proclamation."

When King Edward VIII renounced his throne for Wallis Warfield, he entered into a MORGANATIC marriage. Such a marriage is one in which a man of royal rank marries a woman of lower degree, and the wife and children do not share the husband's rank or the property pertaining to it. Because such property could not be inherited, it became the custom for the husband to present his wife with a gift the morning after their marriage. This was known as the "morning gift" and from its German equivalent, *Morgengabe,* Late Latin developed the phrase *matrimonium ad morganaticam,* "morning gift marriage."

BACHELOR came to us through the Old French *bacheler,* young man, from a Late Latin *baccalarius,* farm laborer. The meaning of this Latin word seems to have been something like "cowhand," from *bacca,* a corruption of *vacca,* cow (VACCINE is from this word, because that used in preventing smallpox is taken from "cows.") During feudal times *bacheler* was applied to a lower vassal and then to a young man aspiring to knighthood. Later the word meant a young "unmarried man" and finally received the meaning of "student." At this stage the Latin form *baccalarius* was erroneously considered to have come from *bacca,* berry, and *laureus,* laurel, and so the word was re-latinized to *baccalaureus,* whence our BACCALAUREATE.

INFLUENZA is an Italian word and takes us back to medieval astrology, since it embodies the ancient belief that epidemics are the result of the INFLUENCE of the stars. The latter word also was originally a term of astrology and referred to the supposed "flowing" (Latin *influere,* to flow in) from the stars of an ethereal fluid which governed our characters and our fates. The same belief was responsible for the word DISASTER. ASTER is the Greek word for "star" and the flower of this name is a "star-flower." According to astrology, if the stars were against us, the result could only be DISASTER. We still speak

of an "ill-starred" venture. Even the adjective DISMAL seems
to have come from the superstitions of Egyptian astrologers.
We got the word through the Old French *dis mal*, from Latin
dies mali, evil days. This Latin phrase, however, was apparently substituted for an earlier *dies Ægyptiaci*, Egyptian days,
referring to two days of the month which, according to
astrologers, were unfavorable for starting a journey, or, in fact,
for starting any project at all.

HAZARD calls up a picture of soldiers, bored to death during
the long siege of the Castle of Hasart in Palestine, at the time
of the Crusades. As soldiers are wont to do in such circumstances, these besiegers whiled away the time in gambling,
and one of them invented a new game which they christened
hasard. From this old French game of chance our modern
craps is derived, and from it likewise arises naturally enough
our use of the word HAZARD. Gambling is indeed a HAZARDOUS
occupation, whether it be craps or the stock market!

The Crusades were also responsible for the word RENEGADE,
which came into English from the Spanish *renegado*, one
who has "denied" his faith — and turned Mohammedan when
captured, as many did to secure better treatment. The source
of the word is the Latin *re-negare*, to deny, which also gives
us RENEGE or "renig," a crime among bridge players.

ASSASSIN is another word brought back to Europe by the
Crusaders, and derives from the Arabic *Hashshashin*, literally
"hashish eaters." This was a XIIIth century sect of murderous
Mohammedan fanatics, who acted under the influence of
hashish, an oriental narcotic made from Indian hemp.

THUG is similarly derived. This word is the Hindustani *thag*,
which referred to a member of an organization of religious
assassins who were bound to secret murder in the service of
Kali, the Hindu goddess of destruction. This fierce sect was
suppressed by the British early in the last century.

A HALL MARK was the stamp used by the Goldsmiths' Hall in
London, certifying the quality of gold and silver articles. The

term no longer makes much sense when we are assured that every trade mark is the "HALL MARK of quality," whether it concern cigarettes, handkerchiefs, or automobiles. A similar extension of meaning has taken place with the word STERLING, originally applied only to coins.

It was once the custom to put toasted bread in liquor. We now take our champagne straight and confine our dunking largely to doughnuts and coffee, but we still drink a TOAST to our friends!

Our words for expressing lineal measurements show that the early groping in this respect would hardly satisfy the Bureau of Standards. Only INCH had any very definite meaning and because it is interesting for another reason, this word will be reserved for a later chapter. FOOT was of necessity only an approximation, while YARD is the Anglo-Saxon *gyrd*, stick, pole. The same word is used for a "pole" across a ship's mast. Five and one-half YARDS make a ROD, a POLE, or a PERCH. The latter word came to us through the Old French *perche*, from the Latin *pertica*, a pole. Forty RODS are equivalent to one FURLONG or "furrow-long," the length of a plowed furrow in a field, and eight FURLONGS give us a MILE. This word was introduced into Anglo-Saxon in very early times from the Latin *milia* (*passum*), a thousand (paces), and was once considerably less precise than 5280 feet.

Early pennies in England were square and marked with a cross so that they could be cut into quarters. One of these quarter-pennies was a FARTHING ("fourth-ing"). The ending was a diminutive, found also in SHILLING and "penning," the earlier form of PENNY. King Edward I, however, in order to avoid fraud, had round pennies made and reduced their weight to a "standard" of thirty-two grains of wheat, taken from the center of the ear—whence the origin of PENNYWEIGHT.

The present meaning of PIAZZA arose in connection with the building of Covent Garden in London in the XVIIth century. The Garden was laid out as a "square" in the Italian fashion, with arcades running along two sides. The Square was named "Covent Garden PIAZZA," and because the arcades were the novel part of the arrangement, Londoners transferred the meaning of PIAZZA to them. The word still means "arcade" in England, but in the United States we have extended the meaning further to "verandah," which, to be sure, is a sort of arcade. PIAZZA is an Italian word and means exactly what it was intended to mean at Covent Garden: "square." French *place* and Spanish *plaza* have the same sense, and all these words go back through Latin to the Greek phrase *plateia* (*hodos*), broad (way). As used in English, PLACE had originally this same sense, but the meaning of the word has now become so extended and generalized as to mean almost anything.

We now differentiate between STATIONERY and STATIONARY, but the two are really one. What possible connection can there be between writing paper and, for example, a STATIONARY engine? For this we must look back to the days of primitive trading when most selling was done by wandering hucksters. It would seem that the first to free themselves from pushcarts and to start up business in a STATIONARY location, were the booksellers, who probably started with stalls similar to those today along the Seine in Paris. These booksellers then became STATIONERS, since they had a STATION or fixed location for selling their wares. Because books and writing materials were frequently sold together, some confusion arose, and eventually the STATIONER began to concentrate on writing materials alone.

Another tradesman who has come up in the world is the BROKER. He used to be the "broacher," one who "broached" or "opened" a cask of wine and sold it at retail. The word stems ultimately from a Latin *broca,* pointed spike, which also gave BROOCH (a pin). Now we may even BROACH a subject, though we do not often need a pointed spike for the purpose.

The word SCAVENGER looks as though it might have come

to us from Latin through the medium of French. It resembles, for instance, the word "messenger," which we have borrowed from the French. Actually, however, SCAVENGER derives from the Anglo-Saxon *sceawian*, which meant "to see," "to scrutinize," and which has now become our verb SHOW. The earliest form of SCAVENGER was "scawageour," and the word meant "customs officer," one to whom it was necessary to "show" merchandise for customs inspection. The present meaning arises from the fact that early customs officers were also street cleaners!

LIMELIGHT goes back to the days before incandescent bulbs, when the only means of getting a brilliant spotlight in a theatre was by playing upon "lime" an intensely hot flame produced by burning a mixture of oxygen and hydrogen under pressure. A word that takes us much further back into theatrical history is MATINÉE, which is the French word for "morning." Why should this word be used for an "afternoon performance"? In the days of candles, it was simply impossible to properly illuminate a theatre with artificial light. Regular theatrical performances were therefore presented in the afternoon and any extra shows were given in the "morning." When lighting methods improved and plays could be given in the evening, the MATINEE moved over into the afternoon. The name stuck, however, and it still remained a "morning show."

We do not have much accurate information concerning the early Greek theatre. We do know, however, that early Greek plays were sung, and this fact is confirmed in the derivation of both COMEDY and TRAGEDY. The second element of both words is the Greek *aoide*, song (from which we also get the word ODE). COMEDY meant "revel (Greek *komos*) song" and TRAGEDY "goat (*tragos*) song." It is thought that actors in Greek tragedies may have dressed in goat skins to represent satyrs.

A SARCOPHAGUS is literally a "flesh-eater" and owes its formation to an old Greek superstition. The word is a compound of the Greek *sarkos,* flesh, and *phagein,* to eat. The ancient Greeks believed that a certain limestone, used especially for coffins, had the property of reducing the flesh to dust. We quite fittingly speak of "biting SARCASM," for this word comes from the Greek *sarkazein,* to tear flesh, and so likewise goes back to *sarkos.*

For the origin of SCAPEGOAT we must go to the Bible. Among the ancient Jews, the SCAPEGOAT was chosen by lot on the Day of Atonement. We find the story behind this word in the sixteenth chapter of Leviticus:

And the Lord said unto Moses: "Speak unto Aaron thy brother, that . . . he shall take two goats, and present them before the Lord at the door of the tabernacle . . . And Aaron shall cast lots upon the two goats; one lot for the Lord, and the other for the SCAPEGOAT. And Aaron shall bring the goat upon which the Lord's lot fell, and offer him for a sin offering. But the goat, on which the lot fell to be the SCAPEGOAT, shall be presented alive before the Lord, to make an atonement with him, and to let him go for a SCAPEGOAT into the wilderness . . . And Aaron shall lay both his hands upon the head of the live goat, and confess over him all the iniquities of the children of Israel, and all their transgressions in all their sins, putting them upon the head of the goat, and shall send him away by the hand of a fit man into the wilderness: and the goat shall bear upon him all their iniquities unto a land not inhabited . . . And this shall be an everlasting statute unto you, to make an atonement for the children of Israel for all their sins once a year." And he did as the Lord commanded Moses.

Despite its widespread use today (the word has even been adopted into French), FOLKLORE is of very recent origin. The expression was coined in England only a hundred years ago, in 1846, by W. J. Thoms. LORE is from the old Anglo-Saxon *lar,* teaching, doctrine. In this connection, it is interesting to note that such a sedate word as LEARNED is a corruption of what in Chaucer's time was "lered" ("taught," not "learned"), also from the noun *lar.* This word is a LEARNED cousin of the untutored "I'll learn you"!

HOMESICK is another fairly recent addition to our "word treasure." This word is attributed to Coleridge, who in 1798 wrote a poem by that name, and is a translation of the German *Heimweh*. The German word originated in Switzerland, where it first appears in medical literature of the XVIIth century, referring to an actual sickness experienced by people used to high altitudes, when they came down to live in the valleys.

BRAGGADOCIO is a man-made word, but is somewhat older than FOLKLORE and HOMESICK. This word was coined by Spenser in the XVIth century for a boastful character in his "Faërie Queene." He simply added an imitative Italian ending to the word "brag."

A great deal of nonsense has been written about the origin of curious place names, both in America and elsewhere. When traced down realistically, many of these tales turn out to be more legendary than historical. The name POMFRET, however, is interesting. While there is not much historical fact on which to base its derivation, the origin of this name seems clear linguistically. As happened in the naming of most New England towns, this Connecticut village took its name from a town in England. The English POMFRET was spelled "Pontefract" and the name was derived from the Latin phrase (*ad*) *pontem fractum*, (at) the broken bridge. For such a name to have stuck, it would seem that an old Roman bridge located there must have lain in ruins for many generations.

Chapter V

WHAT'S IN A WORD?

MANY words take on more interest and flavor if we look into the literal meanings of their component parts, and if we go back to see from just what ancient words they were derived. Such early meanings, while not often applicable today, give us a clearer and more concrete picture of the words we use in everyday speech.

Caesar, for example, was AMBITIOUS and he got that way by "going about" (Latin *ambire*) to solicit votes for office, as do most candidates today. CANDIDATES were so named because of the "white" (Latin *candidus*) togas which, in ancient Rome, office seekers wore in order to distinguish themselves.

AMETHYST is a Greek word meaning "not drunk." This stone was considered by the ancients to be a talisman against the vice of drinking.

ANECDOTE is another Greek word and meant "things unpublished." Possibly Greek ANECDOTES were of the variety not suitable for publication!

An AVALANCHE falls down "into the valley" (French *à val*). The French also take things "down into the valley" when they swallow, for "to swallow" is the meaning of the French verb *avaler!*

There might be a slight question as to which comes first in the derivation of BOWEL from the Late Latin *botulus*, sausage! Modern scientists have again called upon the word to describe BOTULISM, a virulent food poisoning caused by eating bad "sausage," among other things. The bacterium causing this poisoning has been named BOTULINUS, "little sausage." As a matter of fact, this appellation is more appropriate than "bacillus" for this whole class of bacteria, because they resemble strings of "little sausages" much more than they do "rods," the meaning of the Latin *bacillus*. In addition to BOWEL, we have the synonym INTESTINES, and this word means quite literally "insides"! The Latin adjective *intestinus* meant "internal," and we still have this meaning in the phrase "INTESTINE war." Even in Latin times, the *canalis intestinus* was the "inside canal."

When we see the word CARDINAL, we are apt to think of a certain red color, but this meaning has arisen solely from the red robes worn by CARDINALS of the Roman Catholic Church.

CARDINALS in turn were so-called because they were originally in charge of the principal or CARDINAL churches in Rome. The same sense of "chief" or "principal" occurs in CARDINAL sins or virtues, CARDINAL points, etc. The word has this idea of "chief" because it is derived from the Latin *cardo,* hinge — "that on which a thing turns," hence, "that which is of chief importance."

Have you ever thought of a CHENILLE bedspread as "crawling with caterpillars"? Perhaps I shouldn't have mentioned it, but this word means "caterpillar" in French!

A COMPANION is etymologically "someone you eat bread with." We have the word through Old French from a Late Latin *companionem,* a compound of *cum,* with, and *panis,* bread.

A CONCLAVE is quite literally a "lockup." This is a Latin word meaning "a room that may be locked up *with* a *key*" (from *cum,* with, and *clavis,* key). The word was used for the room in which cardinals are "locked up" during the election of a pope, then for the meeting itself, and later for any secret meeting.

It is easy to see why CONGLOMERATION has come to mean "hodgepodge," "mess," or "tangle," when we know that this word is composed of the Latin *cum,* together, and *glomus,* ball of yarn. *Glomus* is akin to *globus,* globe, ball, and the dictionary even lists a word CONGLOBATION.

When we become DECREPIT, we literally "creak" with age (Latin *crepitare,* to creak or crack). CREVICE is a related word and means a "crack." While on the subject of old age, we may note that the Roman SENATE was a council of "old men" (Latin *senex,* old man, which has also given us SENIOR and SENILE).

A farmer who cannot plow a straight furrow is actually DELIRIOUS, whatever be the reason for his unsteadiness. The Latin verb *delirare* meant "to depart from a straight furrow (*lira*)" and hence figuratively "to go astray in one's mind."

The verb to DERIVE, with which you surely have become thoroughly acquainted by now, "derives" from the Latin *derivare,* to draw off water from a stream (*de-*, away from, and *rivus,* stream). Even in ancient times, however, the word had developed its modern sense. The idea is that of "drawing (a word) downstream (from its source)." RIVAL is a closely related word. The Latin adjective *rivalis* meant simply "belonging to a stream." Used as a noun, the word meant "one who uses a stream in common with another," and from this sense there developed the meaning of "a near neighbor," without any reference to a stream. When Shakespeare writes "the RIVALS of my watch" (in Hamlet), the meaning is clearly "sharers" or "companions." *Rivalis* then took on the figurative sense of "one who has the same mistress as another," in other words, "a RIVAL in love." ARRIVE looks as though it might have a similar derivation, but this word developed through French from a Late Latin *arripare,* to come "to shore," to land. The compound was formed from *ad,* to, and *ripa,* bank, shore. Etymologically, then, we may ARRIVE by boat, but not by train.

DESSERT is a French word meaning "what comes after the table has been cleared." This noun was formed from the verb *desservir,* to clear the table, literally "to de-serve."

A DILAPIDATED building is one that is falling apart "stone by stone." The derivation is from Latin *di-*, apart, and *lapis,* stone, from which we also get LAPIDARY, a dealer in precious "stones."

EFFRONTERY was formed on the Latin adjective *effrons,* shameless, which in turn is composed of the prefix *e(x)-*, without, and *frons,* forehead. The "forehead" was considered by the ancients to be the seat of "shame." The sense of *frons* was eventually extended to mean the FRONT of anything.

ELIMINATE is a compound of the Latin prefix *e-*, out of, and *limen,* threshold. The original sense was "to turn out of doors," "to kick across the threshold." Psychology has adopted LIMEN as the "threshold" of consciousness, the point at which a reaction to a stimulus becomes perceptible.

An EPIDEMIC is a disease that spreads quickly "among the people." Here we have the Greek *epi,* among, upon, and *demos,* people.

FOOL derives quite understandably from the Latin *follis,* bellows, wind-bag! The related FOLLICLE means a small "bag" or "gland" in the body.

FORCEPS is the Latin word for "tongs" and seems to have meant "the thing taking hold of that which is hot," from *formus,* hot, and *capere,* to take. FURNACE is a related word, from Latin *fornacem,* furnace.

A hand GRENADE reminded the Spaniards of a "pomegranate" because it is filled with shrapnel as the fruit is filled with seeds. The Spanish *grenada,* from which GRENADE is derived, means "pomegranate" and is from the Latin *granata,* seeded, full of seeds (from *granum,* grain, seed). GARNET owes its name to the French form of the same word: *grenat.* The stone was so named because of its resemblance to the red pomegranate seed. (POMEGRANATE is a compound with Latin *pomum,* apple.)

Our spelling of GROCER has obscured the original meaning. This word is the Old French *grossier,* one who sells in the "gross," a wholesale dealer.

HYDROPHOBIA is composed of the Greek words *hudor*, water, and *phobos,* fear, and the disease is so called because it is accompanied by an abnormal "fear of water." RABIES, another name for the same disease, is simply the Latin word for "madness."

INEXORABLE means literally "not to be moved by prayer" and was formed from the Latin negative *in-* plus *exorare,* to speak out, to entreat. PRECARIOUS shows that the Romans were not altogether convinced of the efficacy of "prayer," for this is the Latin *precarius,* doubtful, literally "obtained by prayer," from *precari,* to pray. An IMPRECATION is a "prayer" of sorts, an appeal to the gods to bring down evil upon someone, a curse.

INSIDIOUS means "lying in wait," or, quite literally, "sitting in wait." The Latin adjective *insidiosus* already had our modern meaning, but was formed from the noun *insidiae,* ambush. The ultimate root is the verb *sedere,* to sit. The etymology of the word AMBUSH itself shows us where such a "sitting in wait" was most likely to take place: the Old French verbal form was *embuscher,* from the Late Latin *imboscare,* composed of *in-,* in, and *boscus,* woods. So the "sitting in wait" takes place "in the woods." BOUQUET is a related French word, from the Italian diminutive *boschetto,* little bush. Another word, that has long since lost the sense of "ambush" for a more romantic meaning, is TRYST. In Old French, as *triste* or *tristre,* this word meant either "ambush" or simply "a station in hunting" — a place where you sit and wait for someone to send a deer past. From the deer's point of view, however, this too could only be interpreted as an ambush!

If you are INTELLIGENT, you are able to "choose between" two things wisely. This is a compound of the Latin *inter,* between, and the verb *legere,* which meant first "to pick," to gather, to collect, then "to pick out carefully," to choose, to select, and finally "to pick out with the eyes," to read. From these several meanings we get such varied words as LEGUME, a plant to be "picked," LEGION, originally a body of troops levied or "chosen," LEGEND, something "to be read," LESSON, a "reading" (the word still has this meaning in church services), and LEGIBLE, "readable."

INTERVAL is made up of the Latin words *inter,* between, and *vallum,* wall. The original meaning was "the space between two walls."

If you grow LETTUCE in your garden, you know that the stem contains a milky juice, and this juice has given the word its name. The Latin form was *lactuca,* from *lactem,* milk, from which we also get LACTIC acid.

MALARIA is simply Italian for "bad air." It was known that this disease occurred mainly in low, marshy country; but until doctors discovered that the mosquito breeding in these swamps was the real culprit, people assumed that the fever was produced by harmful vapors arising from such marshy land.

We are now apt to think of a MANUFACTURED article as opposed to a "hand-made" one. To MANUFACTURE, however, is literally "to make by hand" (Latin *manu,* hand, and *facere,* to make). We find the same idea again in MANUSCRIPT, something "written by hand," and in MANUAL, a "handbook."

The verb to MUSE is derived from the same source as MUZZLE. Both go back to a Latin *musus,* snout. The idea of "dreaming" in MUSE has come from the way a dog sniffs the air with his "snout" when he is doubtful about a scent.

If anything is OBVIOUS, it is "in the middle of the road," for everyone to see. This word is compounded from Latin *ob-,* on, and *viam,* way, road. DEVIOUS means "out-of-the-way" (Latin *de-,* out of, and *viam,* way), and TRIVIAL means "commonplace," literally "pertaining to the crossroads." The Latin noun *trivium* meant "a place where three roads meet" (*tri,* three, and *viam,* road).

An ONION, believe it or not, is really "a pearl of great price." The Latin *unionem* (from *unus,* one) referred specifically to a "single" large pearl, just as we use "solitaire" today, usually in reference to a diamond. UNION is, of course, the same word and means "oneness."

OVAL means "egg-shaped," and this is precisely its derivation, from the Latin *ovum,* egg. We have the word again in OVARY.

When the PIANO was perfected, its inventor anounced that he had a harpsichord which could play *piano e forte,* Italian for "soft and loud." The instrument then came to be known as the PIANOFORTE, which was later shortened to PIANO.

A POMMEL is properly a "little apple," and the word came to us through the Old French *pomel* from Latin *pomellus,* a diminutive of *pomum,* apple. *Pomel* was applied to any "apple-like" knob, and hence means a "knob-like" projection on a saddle, or a "knob" on a sword hilt. Since a sword was used for "beating," we have also the verb to POMMEL or to PUMMEL.

If an idea is PREPOSTEROUS, it is actually "hindside before." Here we have a Latin compound of *prae-posterus,* before-behind.

A RECALCITRANT mule is one that "kicks back" — from Latin *re-calcitare,* formed on *calcem,* heel.

A rather obvious compound is RECOIL, which corresponds to the French *reculer,* from Latin *re-* and *culus,* buttocks (the modern French word for which is *cul*).

RETORT is from the Latin *retortus,* past participle of *retorquere,* to twist back. A RETORT may be a reply "twisted back" at someone, or, in the chemistry laboratory, a "twisted" tube or vessel.

While the two words have developed rather different connotations, REVEAL is a literal equivalent to UNVEIL. Both words stem from the Latin *velum,* veil.

REVENUE is "what comes back," sometimes to you, but all too frequently to the government. This word is simply the past participle of the French verb *revenir,* to come back. We also speak of the RETURNS from an investment, using the same concept, while even the word INCOME contains the same idea.

Another French past participle which we use as a noun is ROUÉ. This is from the verb *rouer,* to break on the "wheel" (*roue*). A ROUÉ is a person who deserves this fearful fate.

If you should break your wife's pet dish, she might very well ask you to SCRUTINIZE the result and pick up the pieces. This word is from the Latin *scruta,* broken pieces, and the sense is that of "searching carefully" (even to finding all the "broken pieces").

We now have four SEASONS, but the word, which we received through the Old French *seison,* from Latin *sationem,* originally referred only to Spring. In Classical Latin, *sationem* meant "the act of sowing," but in Late Latin times the word came to mean "the time or SEASON of sowing." A related word is

SEMINARY, originally a "seed-plot," and now a place where "seeds of learning" are sown.

If your job is a SINECURE, you should be "without a care" (Latin *sine cura*).

A SOLDIER is really a "solider" and should be paid in "solid" money. Roman SOLDIERS were mercenaries and the word *soldarius* was invented for them in Late Latin times, deriving from *solidus,* a piece of money. There was actually a coin called the *solidus* at the time of the Late Roman Empire, and it got its name from the phrase *nummus solidus,* solid coin. The French *sou,* penny, is derived from this word and was written and pronounced *sol* in Old French. The British symbol *s.* for "shilling" stands not for "shilling" at all, but for "solidus," just as *d.* is for the Latin *denarii* and £ for *librae.* The word SOLDER is also derived from *solidus;* we use SOLDER to make things "solid."

SOLEMN is from the Latin *solemnis,* for an earlier *sollennis,* which was composed of *sollus,* whole, and *annus,* year. The original meaning was "taking place when the year is complete." The sense of "religious" or SOLEMN derives from "annual" religious festivals.

A SUPERCILIOUS individual is a "highbrow," one who goes around with "raised eyebrows," for this is exactly what the word means. Latin *supercilium* meant "eyebrow" (literally, an "over-eyelid").

A SURGEON must of necessity be "skilled with his hands," and this fact led to the formation of the word SURGERY in ancient Greece. The Greek *kheirourgia* meant precisely "skill with the hands" and was compounded from *kheir,* hand, and *ergein,* to work.

If you have ever heard TERMITES at work, you will agree that the Romans aptly named them "grind-worms." The Latin noun *termitem* was formed from the verb *terere,* to grind or rub. The past participle of the same verb gave us TRITE. A TRITE remark is one that has been "rubbed" until it is worn out.

A TERSE remark is also one that has been "rubbed," but in this case, "rubbed to a high polish." TERSE means literally "polished" and is from *tersus,* the past participle of the Latin verb *tergere,* to polish. POLITE likewise has the meaning of "polished" and was derived from *polire,* the source of the word POLISH itself.

TOIL and TRIBULATION take us back to ancient machines where "foot-power" and "elbow-grease" were prime considerations. TOIL is the Anglo-French *toiler,* to strive, which in turn is a shortening of the Latin *tudiculare,* to stir, from *tudicula,* a machine for bruising olives. Similarly, TRIBULATION comes from the Latin *tribulum,* a threshing sledge. In much the same way, TURMOIL is thought to come from the Old French *tremouille,* a mill hopper, appropriately derived from the Latin verb *tremere,* to shake.

When a medium purports to go into a TRANCE, she claims to "go beyond" into the realm of the dead. The word comes from the Old French verb *transir,* to depart, to die, a compound formed from the Latin *trans,* beyond, and *ire,* to go. We have many words whose derivation from this source is more obvious: TRANSIENT, TRANSIT, TRANSITION, TRANSITORY, etc. To TRESPASS likewise means to "go beyond" and in Old French *trespasser* also meant "to die," to "pass away." This verb was formed with the Late Latin *passare,* to go, instead of with the classical *ire.*

The street URCHIN owes his name to the Old Norman French word *herichun,* which came from the Latin *ericius,* hedgehog. The sea URCHIN is a shellfish related to the starfish and having a globe-like shell covered with long spines.

VINEGAR was quite accurately named "sour wine." The French form of the word is *vinaigre,* a compound of *vin,* wine, and *aigre,* sour.

Not many of us would connect the verb to VISIT with such words as VISION, VISIBLE, VISUAL, etc., but they all go back to *visus,* the past participle of the Latin verb *videre,* to see. Latin had already formed the verb *visitare* and it meant "to go and *see*," to VISIT.

So far we have been concerned in this chapter with interesting derivations from Greek and Latin sources. There are also some good old Anglo-Saxon words that become more meaningful when we delve into their backgrounds.

AFTERMATH, for example, was originally a farm term and meant literally an "after-mowing," a second mowing (from Anglo-Saxon *mæth*, mowing).

A FOSTER mother is one who "feeds" or nurses a child not her own. In Anglo-Saxon *fostor* meant "*nourishment*" and was derived from *foda*, food. The meaning has been extended to "care" in general and the related verb to FOSTER has the same sense.

The rather lofty LORD and LADY had very humble origins indeed. Both are shortened forms of ancient Anglo-Saxon words: the LORD was originally the *hlaf-weard* or "loaf-warden," while his LADY was the *hlaf-dige* or "loaf-kneader." The shortening process in both words is not as complicated as it may seem: hlafweard — hlaweard — laward — lord, and hlafdige — hladige — ladige — ladig — lady.

The numbers ELEVEN and TWELVE are interesting because they both contain an old Teutonic root *lif*, which had the sense of "to leave." When primitive man had counted the ten fingers of his two hands, he was at a loss, and the best he could do was to say "one left over" (ELEVEN) and "two left over" (TWELVE)! After he had once achieved this hurdle, he got the idea of saying "three-ten," "four-ten," etc.

A STIRRUP or "sty-rope" is a "mounting-rope," from Anglo-Saxon *stigan*, to rise, to mount, to climb — the same word as the German *steigen*. A STY on the eye is likewise a "rising" and derives from the same verb.

When you next ask for a price on having a chair "re-done," you may quite fittingly tell the UPHOLSTERER: "It's a hold-up!" The early form of this word was "upholdster," one who "holds up" goods for inspection. The ending *-ster* is the same feminine form found in TEAMSTER, WEBSTER, etc. (see page 34).

Chapter VI

AS THE TWIG IS BENT

READ carefully the following sentence and see what it means to you: "One touch of nature makes the whole world kin." Ten to one that, unless you are thoroughly versed in Shakespeare, you will visualize beautiful sunsets, walks in the woods, waves pounding on a rock-bound coast, etc., etc. The quotation is from *Troilus and Cressida*, Act III, Scene 3:

> One touch of nature makes the whole world kin,
> That all, with one consent, praise new-born gauds.

What Shakespeare meant, when he wrote these lines, was that "all men are alike in one natural characteristic — that they all, without exception, fall for newfangled notions." Until the Romantic movement of the early XIXth century, the word NATURE did not have the connotations which it has for us today.

As we saw in Chapter I, language is dynamic, and words undergo a continuous process of growth and change of meaning. Sometimes a word develops a new meaning very gradually, while in other cases a new concept is forced upon a word quite suddenly, as happened to BROADCAST with the advent of the radio industry. An adequate treatment of this phase of word study is beyond the scope of this little book. In this chapter I shall discuss a few words that have undergone shifts in meaning of particular interest. Some of these changes are readily explained, while others are only a matter of conjecture.

A good example with which to start off is HUMOR, the Latin

word for "liquid." It is a far cry from this old Latin word to the HUMOR of Mark Twain and Bennett Cerf. The evolution of the word starts with the physiology of the ancients, who attributed to the body four kinds of "humors" or "liquids": blood, phlegm, bile, and melancholy or "blackbile." If these "humors" were not properly balanced, and a man had too much blood, he was SANGUINE (from Latin *sanguinem,* blood), if he had too much phlegm, he was PHLEGMATIC, an over-supply of bile made him BILIOUS, and an excess of melancholy caused him to be MELANCHOLY. The balancing or "tempering" of the "humors" was a man's TEMPERAMENT, and when this balance became greatly disturbed, the result was DISTEMPER. The word COMPLEXION was once synonymous with TEMPERA-MENT and indicated the way in which a man's constitution was "woven together" (Latin *cum,* together, and *plectere,* to weave). Since a person's TEMPERAMENT could be determined, to some extent at least, by the color and texture of the face, COMPLEXION gradually assumed the latter meaning. Now an excess of any of these four "humors" might make a man odd, eccentric, funny, HUMOROUS. From this sense it was not a great step for HUMOR to come to mean "the capacity of perceiving the odd or incongruous." Of course we can still be in a "bad HUMOR," and the dictionary still gives "irritable" as one mean-ing of HUMOROUS. WIT has had a somewhat similar history, for this word originally meant "intellect." We still say, "Keep your WITS about you."

The verb to STOP looks like an old Anglo-Saxon word, and indeed it was. Nevertheless, this word was introduced very early from Latin, and was derived from the Latin noun *stuppa,* oakum. Men have used this material from time immemorial for calking or STOPPING the seams of wooden boats, in order to STOP the water from pouring through. In my log-cabin summer home I too used *stuppa* to STOP the cracks between the logs in order to STOP the air (and, more important, the mosquitoes) from pouring through. The French adopted this word from English, first as a sea-term with the sense of "stop her!" when docking a ship. They later began to use the word for trains and automobiles.

COPY is the Latin *copia* which meant "abundance," as is obvious from our words COPIOUS and CORNUCOPIA, the "horn of plenty." From the noun was formed a verb which meant "to make an abundance," "to multiply"; but of course we can multiply by one as well as by many. So we now speak of "a COPY," without any thought of "abundance."

Although you will still find the original meaning in the dictionary, RESTIVE, as we use the word today, has come to be synonymous with RESTLESS. The two are actually opposites. First, we should have clearly in mind that there are two separate words in English, both spelled R-E-S-T. The one, meaning "quiet" or "peace" is an Anglo-Saxon word, but the other, which means "remainder" or "what is left," came to us through the Old French *reste*, from the Latin *re-stare*, to stand back, to hang back, to remain. This latter word is the source of RESTIVE, from Old French *restif*. In modern French the word is spelled *rétif* and has retained its meaning of "stubborn," "unwilling to go forward," the sense which our English word should properly have. RESTLESS, on the other hand, from Anglo-Saxon *rest*, means "finding no repose," "always active or in motion." Because of the confusion that has arisen between these two words, the phrase "a RESTIVE horse" may now mean "a stubborn horse that will not go," or it may also mean (and now usually does) "an unruly horse that cannot be held back!"

PARBOIL has always been for me a confusing word. Even before I knew its derivation, I always felt that the word meant "to boil thoroughly," and this is indeed exactly what it should mean. PARBOIL is a compound of the Latin *per*, through, and *bullire*, to boil. The original sense of "to boil through and through" shifted to that of "to boil partially" because a confusion arose between the prefix "par-" and the word "part."

Purely by accident then this word too has come to mean the exact opposite of what it once did. PERUSE ("per-use") shows the same construction, but has lost its earlier meaning of "to use up." In PERUSING this page, however, you have quite literally "used up" the printed matter appearing upon it.

A PERTINENT remark is one that is "fitting," one that "pertains" to the subject. Because an IMPERTINENT remark, on the other hand, does "not pertain," the latter word has come to mean "flippant" or "saucy." This change has not occurred, however, in the case of the synonym IRRELEVANT, which still means only "not relevant" or "not pertaining" to the matter at hand. The verb to DISPARAGE has had a similar history. The original meaning is obvious from the noun DISPARITY, which denotes nothing more than "inequality." In Old French, however, the verb *desparagier* took on the specialized meaning of "to *marry* unequally." This use of the word led to the present meanings of "to bring discredit upon" and "to speak slightingly of."

LOZENGES are often "hard as rocks," and this word goes back ultimately to the Latin *lapis*, stone. The relationship, however, is one of shape rather than one of hardness. From Latin the word went into the Provençal language of Southern France as *lausa*, and meant "tombstone." Because these old tombstones were diamond-shaped, *lausa* then passed over into Old French (in the form *losenge*) to mean "a diamond-shaped figure with four equal sides." The term was used in heraldry for such a figure on a coat of arms. The meaning was later extended to anything having this "diamond-shape," such as candy and coughdrops. The relation of the word to the shape was then forgotten, and the transfer was complete.

BUREAU is the French word for "desk" or "office," and its various meanings have come about in a manner similar to that of EXCHEQUER (page 59). In Old French, *burel* meant "a coarse woolen cloth" used especially for table covers. The steps in the evolution of the meaning of this word are: table cover — writing table — desk — a room with a desk, an office — a government BUREAU, composed of several offices with their personnel. In the United States the meaning has been further extended from "a desk with drawers" to "a chest of drawers" for clothing, toilet articles, etc.

The verb to COMFORT originally meant "to strengthen," "to support," and is derived from the Latin *cum,* together, and *fortis,* strong. From "support" the transition to "console" was a natural one. The original sense is preserved in the legal phrase "to give aid and COMFORT to the enemy."

The old French *chansons de geste* were epic poems of the Middle Ages celebrating the exploits of such heroes as Charlemagne, Roland, and countless others. This Old French word *geste* meant "story" or "account of exploits." The word goes back to the Latin phrase (*res*) *gesta,* (things) done. *Gesta* was the past participle of the verb *gerere,* to do. These "things done," however, could and often did become exaggerated and were frequently "laughable," which gives us the transition to the modern meaning of JEST.

The first meaning of TABBY is "watered silk." Because of the wavy effect produced by such material, the word was transferred to a striped cat and later extended to any cat. The derivation goes back through French and Spanish to the Arabic *'attabiy,* the name of a district in Baghdad where the fabric was made.

A modern wardrobe TRUNK is a far cry from a "dug-out" canoe, but the name goes back to the days when a TRUNK was only a crude chest made by hollowing out the "trunk" of a tree.

PREMISE was (and still is) a term of logic. But the PREMISES of a syllogism are quite different from the PREMISES of the man who wants you to keep off them! This word is from the Medieval Latin phrase *praemissa* (*propositio*), (a proposition) "put in front." From its use in logic, the term came to be used in legal documents, with the sense of "the aforesaid," and eventually was used for "the aforesaid houses and lands," the PREMISES, which had been previously mentioned in the PREMISES or introductory statement of a deed.

A friend of mine recently made fun of his wife because she said she was going to "TRY out" some lard, instead of saying she was going to "render" it. This sense is, however, closer to the original meaning of TRY than is the more common meaning of "attempt." TRY comes through Old French *trier* from a Medieval Latin *triare*, to sift, to pick out, and goes back ultimately to the Classical Latin *terere*, to rub, to grind, to thresh. The sense has developed thus: rub — thresh — sift — test, experiment (a "sifting" process) — attempt to find out by experiment — make an effort, attempt, TRY. Similarly, when we TRY a prisoner, we "sift" the evidence. In many of their uses, TRY and TEST are synonymous, and the latter word too has had an interesting history. TEST comes through Old French, from the Latin *testu*, a small earthen pot (related to *testa* — see page 45). The word came to be used for a small cup used in refining, assaying, or TESTING metals.

A HEARSE was originally a "rake" or "harrow" (Old French *herse*, from Latin *hirpex*, rake, harrow), and to REHEARSE meant "to harrow again," hence "to repeat." In England the word HEARSE was applied to a framework with "rake-like" spikes for holding candles over a coffin, and then to the bier or rack on which the coffin was carried. This word BIER, by the way, serves to remind us that we are literally "carried" both as we enter this world and as we leave it. We are BORNE by our mothers until we are BORN (only another spelling of "borne") on the day of our BIRTH; and we are BORNE to our graves on a BIER. All these words go back to the Anglo-Saxon *beran*, to bear, to carry.

NICE has undergone startling changes of meaning in the course of its career. The original sense was "ignorant," and the word comes through Old French from the Latin *nescius*, made up of *ne*, not, and *scire*, to know. In Chaucer's time NICE meant both "stupid" and "weak," while today we give the word such different meanings as "precise" (a NICE distinction) and "pleasing" (a NICE taste). The steps from "weak" to "precise" to "pleasing" are apparent in the word DELICATE: a person may be in DELICATE ("weak") health, and scientists use DELICATE ("precise") instruments. We no longer use DELICATE to mean "pleasing," but the word comes from the Latin *deliciae,* "delight," and we have retained this sense of "pleasing" in the noun DELICACY.

The location of the stomach has fallen considerably since early Greek times. We start out with the Greek word *stoma,* which meant "mouth." "Stomatitis" means "inflammation of the mouth," and "epidemic stomatitis" is the medical term for "hoof-and-mouth disease." The Greeks formed a diminutive *stomakos,* and used this word for "throat." When the Romans took over the word, they used *stomachus* not only for "esophagus," but they took it down one notch further, to what is now properly the STOMACH. We Anglo-Saxons, in our primness, and much to the amusement of Continentals, have taken the poor word down to the bottom rung of the ladder, using it in place of "belly"!

PREVENT comes through the French *prévenir* from Latin *prae-venire,* to come before, to anticipate. If you "come before" an action, you may "get the start of it" and thus PREVENT it. The Latin word itself went through these various stages. The French *prévenir,* however, has taken a different course, and now means "to warn," the idea being that, if you anticipate an action, you are in a position to "warn" against it. When you HINDER an action, on the other hand, instead of "coming before," you try to make it get "behind" schedule, hoping thus to HINDER it (see LET, page 32). IMPEDE and OBSTRUCT run along the same line of thought and are interesting in their derivations. When you IMPEDE anything, you quite literally "put your foot in it." The Latin word was *impedire,* to entangle, to hinder, and was composed of *in,* in, and *pedem,* foot. If you wish to OBSTRUCT the passage of your neighbor from his garden into yours, you "build a STRUCTURE against" him, in order to block the way. Here we have the Latin *obstruere,* to build against. The past participle of *struere* was *structum,* and from it we have other compounds like INSTRUCT, "to build in," and CONSTRUCT, "to build together."

The original meaning of the Latin *virtus,* which gave us VIRTUE, was "manliness" — yet we speak of a "woman's VIRTUE"! The word developed thus: manliness — strength, power — any admirable quality — moral excellence — chastity.

The meaning of UNDERTAKER has become restricted through time. This word once meant "contractor," one who UNDERTAKES a contract, and has also had successively the meanings of "impresario" (Italian for UNDERTAKER) and "publisher." We have taken over the French equivalent *entrepreneur* for "business manager" and now reserve UNDERTAKER for "funeral manager."

GROTESQUE is a French word, borrowed from the Italian *grottesca.* The latter word meant originally "antique work" and referred to the antique style of mural decorations found in excavated chambers or "grottos"; hence the notion of "fantastic" or "extravagant."

DEPART comes through the French *départir* from Latin *de-partire,* to divide. The French word still means "divide," "separate," PARTITION. Its English cousin, however, has taken over the function of the simple French form *partir,* to leave. In the XVIth century this French word also meant "divide" or "separate," but it came to be used reflexively and *se partir* then meant "to separate from each other," hence, to DEPART. The reflexive pronoun *se* was later omitted.

We find the original sense of QUAINT in the compound ACQUAINT. These words stem from Old French *coint* and *acointer,* both of which go back to the Latin *cognitum,* known. The word RECOGNIZE means "to know again" and comes from the same source, by a more direct route. It has been suggested that the sequence for the meaning shift that has taken place in QUAINT is: known — famous — remarkable — strange, odd, QUAINT. While this evolution is both simple and intriguing, I cannot find any justification for it. So far as I am able to discover, the first three steps (known — famous — remarkable) have never appeared in either French or English. The oldest recorded sense in both languages seems to have been "knowing" rather than "known." From the obsolete meanings which the word has been known to have, I would rather develop the sequence thus: knowing — skillful — neat — fastidious — old-fashioned — QUAINT.

If you have cultivated the ability to read French menus, you know that the word *farci* means "stuffed." The original sense of FARCE was precisely "stuffing." A FARCE was a short comedy "stuffed in" between two serious dramas. An INTER-LUDE is similarly something used to fill in "between plays" (Latin *inter,* between, and *ludus,* play).

MINIATURE has come through French and Italian from Latin *miniatus,* the past participle of *miniare,* to paint with red lead (*minium*). The word was used for the illuminations of medieval manuscripts, then for any very small painting, especially portraits on ivory. The meaning was later extended to anything "very small." We doubtless associate the word with the adjective MINUTE, but there is actually no relationship between the two words.

The hard-boiled INFANTRY will hardly appreciate the history of this word. INFANTRY and INFANT have the same source in the Latin *infantem,* unspeaking. The word referred first to a baby that had not yet learned to talk. INFANT later assumed the meaning "boy," with the sense of "servant," and in the Middle Ages this word was applied to a knight's "attendants," those who formed his INFANTRY.

SHAMBLES has been in our language a long time, but was derived from the Latin *scamellum,* little bench. The evolution of the meaning is quite clear: bench — butcher's bench — butcher shop — slaughter house — any place of carnage or destruction. RAMSHACKLE has in it a similar idea, and stands for an earlier "ransackled." A "ransackled" house was one that had been RANSACKED. The latter word is an Old Norse compound of "house" (*rann*) and "search" (*sack*, akin to "seek").

There are other words of Anglo-Saxon origin that have undergone curious changes of meaning in the course of the history of our language. The phrase BY AND BY, for instance, meant in the first place "side by side," from the Anglo-Saxon *bi*, near. We still use BY in this sense when we say "the chair BY the window." The meaning of BY AND BY, however, has shifted from place to time. We make much the same shift when we say, "he did it *on the spot*," while if we say instead, "he did it *then and there*," we employ both place and time concepts simultaneously. The word NEXT similarly means "nearest" in either time or place.

FREE comes from an old Teutonic root meaning "dear," and thus we get from it the related word FRIEND. The present sense of FREE arose from the distinction between the members of the *family* — those who were FREE ("dear") because of kinship — and those who were not thus FREE, the slaves.

The original meaning of NAUGHTY (from "naught") was either "destitute" (having "naught") or "wicked" (good for "naught"). In Shakespeare the word is synonymous with "wicked," and we now find this use of NAUGHTY incongruous, since we reserve the term for children.

The word PRETTY has wandered far from its original sense of "crafty." PRETTY is the adjectival form of the Anglo-Saxon noun *prætt*, meaning "trick." So you see even the Anglo-Saxons enjoyed looking at a "tricky number!" CUNNING and CUTE have taken a similar course, though both may still mean "crafty." CUNNING is from Anglo-Saxon *cunnan*, to know (see UNCOUTH, page 37), and meant "knowing," "skillful," "crafty," while CUTE is only a shortened form of ACUTE, from Latin *acutus*, sharp.

GOSSIP has curiously degenerated in exactly the same way

as its French and German cousins (French *compère* and *commère,* and German *Gevatter*). All of these words were originally translations into the vernacular of the Church Latin *compater* and *commater,* "godfather" and "godmother." The Anglo-Saxon form of GOSSIP was *godsibb,* a person "akin to God," from *sibb,* akin. Godparents were apt to be "old folks," and old folks, whether French, German, or English are apt to be GOSSIPY, hence the change in meaning.

SILLY and LUST have also degenerated from their earlier meanings of "blessed" and "pleasure," the meanings still preserved in the German *selig* and *Lust.* Similarly, LEWD was once only "of the *lay* people (Anglo-Saxon *læwede*)," as opposed to the clergy. LEWD then took on these meanings: unlearned, ignorant — vicious — sensual. The French word *crétin,* idiot, came from the Latin *christianus,* Christian, and the German *albern,* foolish, originally meant "kindly, friendly."

DOWN would really seem more reasonable if it meant "up," for it comes from the Anglo-Saxon *dun,* hill. Originally, the adverb was "adown," and meant "from the hill."

TURNPIKE once made a great deal more sense than it now does. A TURNPIKE was first of all a military device: a large revolving beam, covered on all sides with huge spikes, and used principally in defense against cavalry. The next meaning was "turnstile," and later the word was used for a toll "gate" of any kind, whether it "turned" or not. TURNPIKE was then applied to a road having a toll gate, and now is used loosely for any main highway.

FOND stands for "fonned," the past participle of an old verb "fonnen," to be foolish. The original meaning of FOND was "foolish," then "foolishly affectionate," after which the sense of "foolish" was lost. FUN seems to have come from the same source.

WHEEDLE has developed quite naturally from the Anglo-Saxon *wædlian,* to be poor, to beg, from *wædl,* poverty.

We may "SPEED the parting guest" without hastening his

departure, for the expression simply means that we wish him every "success." This word is from the Anglo-Saxon *sped*, success.

A HEATHEN was in the first instance simply a dweller on the "heath." The new meaning derived from the fact that those who lived in remote regions were apt to be deprived of religion. The synonym PAGAN developed in exactly the same way from the Latin *paganus,* peasant, countryman, from *pagus,* country. PEASANT has come from this same Latin word, through the French *paysan.*

The idea of "countryman" leads to a whole group of words that indicate a universal, if unjustified, disdain for the "hayseed." BOOR, for example, is from the Anglo-Saxon *(ge)bur*, a peasant, a dweller in a "bower," and is the same word as the German *Bauer,* farmer. Our NEIGHBOR is our "nigh-boor," a friend who lives nearby. The South African BOER gives us the Dutch spelling of the same word. VILLAIN once meant nothing more than "peasant," one who was attached to a "villa" or estate. This word has suffered a similar fate in French, from which we borrowed it. The modern French adjective *vilain* means "ugly." The adjective NAÏVE is a French word meaning "artless," but it came from the Latin *nativus,* NATIVE, one who is "born" in a given locality (from *natus,* born). When city dwellers go to the country on fishing and hunting trips, they often use NATIVE in reference to the local country-folk, giving the word a disparaging slant similar to that implied by NAÏVE. CHURL, from Anglo-Saxon *ceorl,* is another word that once meant only "peasant." A CHURL was originally a member of the lowest class of free men, just above a slave. Similarly, a SAVAGE was a "man of the woods," from a Late Latin *selvaticus,* of the forest. The English HAG and the German *Hexe,* witch, are both related to the word *hedge* and once meant only "a woman of the woods." The history of KNIGHT and KNAVE is instructive as regards the ups and downs of words. The Anglo-Saxon *cniht* and *cnafe* (the same word as the German *Knabe,* boy) both meant "boy" or "youth," the difference being that the KNIGHT was a "boy" in military service while a KNAVE was a "boy" in domestic service. The KNIGHT became in turn a "horseman," a "man of outstanding bravery," and "one admitted to knighthood" because of his prowess. While the KNIGHT was thus ascending the scale, the KNAVE sank lower and lower, from "servant" to "rogue" and "scoundrel." BLACKGUARD has taken a similar course, having once meant "scullions," "kitchen help," those who "guard" the "black" pots and pans.

If one becomes BOORISH and CHURLISH, VILLAINOUS, or NAÏVE from living in the country, so do we imagine that we become URBANE from dwelling in the city (Latin *urbs*). The Latin adjective *urbanus* already had the sense of both URBAN and URBANE. Similarly, a person developed COURTEOUS or COURTLY manners from living at the court. Indeed, the word CIVILIZATION itself actually means "city-fication."

Occasionally a word will change not in its actual meaning so much as in its connotations. We say "from PILLAR to POST" and both words mean fundamentally the same thing. Chaucer, however, could say of a friar that he was "a noble POST unto his order," where we should have to use PILLAR ("a PILLAR of the church").

We have a large group of nouns that were originally adjectives, quite unrelated to their present meanings. The change came about from adjectival phrases in which the noun was eventually omitted. We have already seen a few examples, mentioned in other connections, such as FOREST, from (*silva*) *forestis*, (a wood) "outside," POUND, from (*libra*) *pondo*, (a pound) "in weight," and MILE, from *milia* (*passum*), "a thousand" (paces).

Many such changes have resulted from an adjectival phrase showing the place of origin. The names of most wines, for instance, were thus formed: CHAMPAGNE, from (*vin de*) *Champagne*, (wine from) Champagne — a region in northeastern France; PORT, from *(vino d'O)porto* — a city of Portugal; and, as we have already seen, SHERRY, from *(vino de) Xeres* — a city of Spain. Other examples of a similar nature are: CURRANT, from the French *(raisins de) Corinthe;* DOLLAR, originally a XVIth century coin, the *(Joachims)thaler,* coined in the *Joachimsthal* (the Joachim Valley) in Bohemia; DENIM, from the French *(serge) de Nîmes;* PEACH, through Old French *pesche,* from the Latin *Persicum (malum),* "Persian" (apple); SIENNA (a pigment), from the Italian *(terra di) Siena,* (earth of) "Siena," a town in Italy; SUEDE, from the French *(gants de)* Suède, (gloves from) "Sweden;" and TURQUOISE, from the French *(pierre)* turquoise, "Turkish" (stone).

Other examples of a miscellaneous nature are: BALANCE, from the Latin *(libra) bilanx,* (a scale) "with two pans," from *bi,* two, and *lanx,* pan; BONNET, from the French *(chapeau de) bonet,* (hat of) "bonet," a kind of material; CORVETTE, through French and Spanish from the Latin *corbita (navis),* (ship) "of burden;" HORIZON, from the Greek *horizon (kuklos),* "limiting" (circle); MOB, an abbreviation of the Latin *mobile (vulgus),* "excitable" (crowd) — incidentally, our word THREAT meant "crowd" in Anglo-Saxon; MAXIM, from the Latin *maxima (sententia),* "greatest" (sentence); NOON, from the Latin *nona (hora),* "ninth" (hour), meaning the ninth hour from sunrise, or 3:00 P.M. — when the church service called the "nones" changed to midday, the word NOON changed time along with it; OCCIDENT and ORIENT, from the Latin *(sol) occidentem,* "setting" (sun) and *(sol) orientem,* "rising" (sun); PLANET, from the Greek *(aster) planetes,* "wandering" (star); PROSE, from the Latin *prosa (oratio),* "straightforward" (speech) — as opposed to poetry; TERRIER, from the French *(chien) terrier,* "earth" or "burrow" (dog); VOWEL, through Old French *vouel,* from the Latin *vocalis (littera),* "voiced" (letter); and WHISKY, from the Gaelic *uisge(-beatha),* "water" (of life) — compare the French *eau de vie,* which means exactly the same thing.

Chapter VII

A ROSE BY ANY OTHER NAME

THERE was no "other name" for a rose, even in Shakespeare's day. English had adopted the Latin word *rosa* for this flower, and the native term had been forgotten. As was pointed out in the first chapter, much of the old Anglo-Saxon vocabulary was replaced by French and Latin equivalents. A curious example of what our language might have been like, had it not been for this French and Latin infiltration, is the title of an old Medieval sermon: *Ayenbit of Inwit,* "again-bite of in-wit (knowledge within)." This is a very precise equivalent of our Latinized "remorse of conscience." REMORSE is from the Latin *re-mordere,* to bite again (a MORSEL is a "bite") and CON-SCIENCE is from *con-scire,* to know with (oneself). In the same manner, we use the Latin derived DESTRUCTION for the native "rack," the verb "to COVER" for "to deck," and MEDIATOR for "middler." It is interesting to observe that, while we no longer have the word "inwit," we still use INSIGHT, formed in exactly the same way.

While many old native terms have been lost completely, many others remain alongside their imported would-be usurpers. Thus we find in formal prayers such redundancies as "ACKNOWLEDGE and CONFESS," "PARDON and FORGIVE," "PRAY and BESEECH," "SHIELD and PROTECT," "STEADFAST and FIRM," "ALMIGHTY and OMNIPOTENT." (ALMIGHTY, however, was not originally a native term, but is a translation of the Latin *omni-potentem,* all-powerful. Similarly, GOSPEL, "good-spell," good tidings, was translated from the Latin *evangelium,* good tidings, formed from the Greek *eu,* well, and *aggellos,* mes-senger.) In the formal language of the Law, we find such superfluities as "WILL and TESTAMENT" and "SITUATE and LYING."

Further examples of such pairs of words, the first native and the second borrowed, are: BOARD-TABLE, BOYISH-PUERILE, BUY-PURCHASE, CLEAVE-DIVIDE, DEADLY-MORTAL, DIRTY-SOILED, EARTHLY-TERRESTRIAL, FATHERLY-PATERNAL, FOE-ENEMY, FOLK-PEOPLE, HEAL-CURE, NAKED-NUDE, SHEPHERD-PASTOR, SPEECH-LANGUAGE, STOOL-CHAIR, STREAM-RIVER, TALE-STORY, TEACHER-INSTRUCTOR, WEAPONS - ARMS, WIFE - SPOUSE, WORD - VERB, WRETCHED-MISERABLE, and YEARLY-ANNUAL.

Of particular interest are words which have been compounded in exactly the same way in both English and Latin: BE-HEAD and DE-CAPITATE, BREAK-FAST and the French *déjeuner,* from Latin *dis-* and *jejunium,* fasting, FORE-RUNNER and PRE-CURSOR, FORE-TELL and PRE-DICT, (a)GAIN(st)-SAY and CONTRA-DICT, HEART-Y and CORD-IAL, ILL-SMELLING and MAL-ODOROUS, MANI("many")-FOLD and MULTI-PLIED (PLY, from Latin *plicare,* to fold) — compare the Anglo-Saxon THREE-FOLD, the hybrid THREE-PLY, and the Latin TRI-PLE; OVER-SEE and SUPER-VISE, UN-FRIENDLY and IN-IMICAL, UN-LOAD and EX-ONERATE (compare ONEROUS, burdensome), UN-READABLE and IL-LEGIBLE.

Thus far we have been observing words of similar meanings which have come from two quite different sources, the one from Anglo-Saxon, the other from Latin. Very few of these pairs are exact synonyms and some, like PASTOR and SHEPHERD, have wandered far apart. We now come to another large group of "word pairs" which are properly called "doublets," two different words that have developed from the same parent word.

In some cases this splitting process had already taken place in Latin. MOMENT and MOVEMENT, for instance, are both from the Latin *momentum,* which in turn was a shortened form of an earlier *movimentum,* from *movere,* to move. The Latin *momentum* came to have, as one of its meanings, the sense of "that which just barely *moves* the scales," then "a very small part of anything," and hence "a MOMENT." We have also taken over this Latin word for the technical term MOMENTUM. MUSCLE and MUSSEL are from Latin *musculus,* a diminutive of *mus,* mouse. The Romans gave both meanings to the word, the one being a "mouse-like" tissue of the body, and the other a "mouse-like" shellfish. OIL is from the Latin *oleum,* oil, which was formed from *olea,* olive. OLIVE itself is from another Latin word *oliva,* OLIVE. *Olea* and *oliva* both go back to the Greek *olaia,* and are simply two forms of the same word. Similarly, with the aid of the prefixes *ex,* away, and *ad,* at, the Romans formed the two words *explodere,* to clap "away," to clap off the stage, to hoot off, and *applaudere,* to clap "at," to applaud. Both words were formed from *plaudere,* to clap. While EXPLODE and APPLAUD should not really be classed as doublets because of the different prefixes, they do neverthe-less show how words split apart.

On the other hand, we have shown the same propensity in English, and we have many doublets that have separated in comparatively recent times, some much earlier than others. CASH is a corruption of CASE, and "a CASH" was once a "money box." These words came through the Old French *casse,* from Latin *capsa,* a box. (Compare CAPSULE, from the Latin diminu-tive *capsula,* a little box.) FANCY is only a contraction of PHANTASY, as is clearly shown from an intermediate form "phantsy." HUMAN and HUMANE have developed quite differ-ent meanings, comparable to the distinction between the adjective KIND and the noun as used in MANKIND and KINDRED; yet HUMAN and HUMANE are two forms of what was once one word. MAIM is a shortened form of MAYHEM, a term of law for the offense of injuring seriously or MAIMING someone. MANGLE comes from an Anglo-French *mahangler,* which seems to have been a variant of the Old French *mahaignier,* to injure. This Old French word is the source of MAYHEM. MANURE is actually an abbreviation of MANEUVER! Both go back to the Old French *manœuvrer,* from a Late Latin *manoperare,* formed on the Classical Latin phrase *manu operari,* to work "by hand." MANEUVER means to "handle" or to MANAGE skillfully, and the verb to MANURE meant originally "to till the soil *by hand,*" from which sense the transition to the idea of "fertilizing" was an easy step.

PERSON and PARSON have both developed through Old French *persone,* person, from the Latin *persona,* the first meaning of which was "mask." From "mask" to "minister" is quite a piece, as they say in New England! The origin of *persona* seems to have been in the verb *per-sonare,* to sound through, and the map of this word's wanderings is somewhat as follows: a thing through which a sound comes — mask — mask used by an actor — character represented by the mask — part or rôle in a play — one who represents a character, an actor (compare *dramatis personae,* the "actors" of the drama) — a representative in general, a PERSON — a representative of the church, a PARSON. HYPOCRITE has a similar derivation, having come from the Greek *hupocrites,* which meant first "interpreter," then "actor," and finally "dissembler."

PORRIDGE is only another form of POTTAGE, from French *potage,* what is in the "pot." SHEAR and SHARE are two forms of the Anglo-Saxon *sceran,* to cut. When something is "cut," it may be SHARED. (The word "divide" means both "to *cut* into parts" and "to SHARE.") Similarly, the SHORE of the sea and a SHORN sheep are variants of *scoren,* the past participle of *sceran.* A SHORE is "cut," broken, and irregular. SHED and SHADE are both from the Anglo-Saxon *scæd* or *scædu,* SHADOW. A SHED makes a SHADOW and thus gives SHADE. SHIRT and SKIRT take us back to the Anglo-Saxon *scyrte,* a SHORT garment, from *scort,* short. STUN is an abbreviated form of ASTONISH, from Old French *estoner,* to stun, to astonish. The French word goes back to the Latin *tonare,* to thunder (compare the modern French *tonnerre,* thunder). To be STUNNED or ASTONISHED is literally "to be struck by a thunderbolt." TUSSLE and TOUSLE both come from a Middle English *tusen,* to pull. And finally, UNKEMPT is a North-English dialect form of UNCOMBED.

By far the largest group of doublets is composed on the one hand of words coming to us from Latin through Old French, a language spoken by the common people and which had developed gradually out of Latin and had suffered great changes in the course of this development; and on the other hand, of words reaching us either directly from Latin or from Latin by way of so-called "learned" French words. I shall make no distinction between the two latter groups. Indeed it is often impossible to tell by which route these "learned" words reached us. Such words were introduced into both English and French by medieval scholars from the Latin of the Church, and again during the period of the Renaissance, this time from Classical Latin.

Some of these French-Latin doublets have retained approximately the same meaning: ABRIDGE-ABBREVIATE, CHASTISE-CASTIGATE, CLERGY-CLERIC, DOUBLE-DUPLEX, FRAIL-FRAGILE, OINTMENT-UNGUENT, PALE-PALLID, PURVEY-PROVIDE, RECOVER-RECUPERATE, ROYAL-REGAL.

Others have drifted apart considerably in usage, but their relationship to each other is still quite clear: APPRAISE-APPRECIATE, ARCH-ARC, CAGE-CAVE, DOUCHE-DUCT, ENVIOUS-INVIDIOUS, FORGE-FABRICATE, FRAY-FRICTION, HOTEL-HOSPITAL, ISOLATE-INSULATE (from *insula,* island), MEDAL-METAL, OBEISANCE - OBEDIENCE, PURSUE - PROSECUTE, RAGE - RABIES, RANSOM-REDEMPTION, RAY-RADIUS, RELEASE-RELAX, SEVER-SEPARATE, SPRITE-SPIRIT, SURE-SECURE, SIR-SENIOR.

Then we find many pairs of words which have become so unlike, both in form and meaning, that we are no longer likely to recognize their relationship to each other. These doublets provide many interesting derivations.

AIM, ESTEEM-ESTIMATE. AIM and ESTEEM are from the Old French words *esmer,* to estimate, and *estimer,* to value, both from the Latin *aestimare,* to estimate, to value. When you AIM, you must ESTIMATE the distance and other factors. The verb "to value" has the meanings of both ESTEEM and ESTIMATE. The latter word came directly from Latin.

AVENGE-VINDICATE. AVENGE reached us through the Old French *avengier* (now *venger*), to take vengeance, to AVENGE, from Latin *ad-vindicare*, to lay claim to, to AVENGE. VINDICATE comes directly from *vindicare* and its present meaning has developed thus: avenge — defend — defend against accusation — clear from a suspicion of dishonor or wrong.

BALM-BALSAM. BALM came through the Old French form *basme* from the Latin *balsamum,* which meant either the fragrant healing gum or BALM of the BALSAM tree, or the tree itself. The sense of BALM was later extended to anything that heals pain, both bodily and mental.

CHANCE-CADENCE. CHANCE is a French word, from a Late Latin *cadentia,* that which "falls out," and specifically, the "falling out" of the dice. The word was formed on the Latin *cadentem,* falling, which is the source of CADENCE. The meaning of CHANCE is obvious; we even say, "It *fell out* by CHANCE." In French the word means "luck," which is even closer to *cadentia.* A CADENCE, on the other hand, is a rhythmic rising and "falling" of sound.

CHAIR-CATHEDRAL. CHAIR comes through the Old French *chaëre* and Latin *cathedra* from the Greek *kathedra,* seat. CATHEDRAL was formed from the Church Latin adjective *cathedralis,* "containing the bishop's throne (*cathedra*)." In modern French the word *chaire* means "pulpit."

CHAMBER-CAMERA. CHAMBER corresponds to the French *chambre,* from the Latin *camera,* vault, room. We took the Latin word itself to describe a CAMERA, which is essentially nothing but a diminutive "dark-room."

DISTRESS-DISTRICT. We have the word DISTRESS from the Old French *destrece,* distress, which came from Latin *districtus,* pulled apart, stretched. When we are DISTRESSED, we are figuratively "stretched," as on the wheel or on some other engine of torture. DISTRICT, coming directly from *districtus,* is a "stretch" of land (compare TRACT, page 52).

EAGER-ACUTE. EAGER is from the French *aigre,* sharp, sour, ACID, and stems from the Latin *acer,* sharp (from *acus,* point, needle). The English "keen" provides a bridge from the idea of "sharp" to that of EAGER. ACUTE comes directly from the Latin *acutus,* sharp, the past participle of *acuere,* to sharpen.

FASHION-FACTION. FASHION is an anglicized version of the French *façon,* which goes back to the Latin *factionem,* a making, a doing, and also "a company of people *doing* something together," a FACTION. The Latin word was formed on the verb *facere,* to make, to do. The notion of FASHION (in all its meanings) arises from the idea of "a way of doing or making."

LODGE-LOBBY. LODGE is the French *loge* and is from a Medieval Latin *lobia,* gallery, which takes us to an Old German word *louba,* arbor (the modern *Laube*). The Italian form *loggia* is closest to the original sense, for it means an "open gallery." LOBBY came more directly from the Latin form and has moved out toward the door of the LODGE. In the United States we have formed the verb to LOBBY because those who wish to "lobby for their hobbies" or for anything else must do so in the outside LOBBIES of Congress.

LOYAL-LEGAL. LOYAL comes through the Old French forms *loial* and *leial* from the Latin *legalem,* formed on the noun *legem,* law. The meaning of LEGAL is clear, while the idea behind LOYAL was "true to the *law,*" hence, "true to one's obligations," "faithful."

MAYOR-MAJOR. MAYOR is an English spelling of the Old French *maiore* (now *maire*), from the Latin *major,* greater. A MAYOR is the "greater" man of a town, while a MAJOR is one of the "greater" men in the army. The adjective MAJOR has retained the original meaning.

RAIL, RULE-REGULATE. RAIL and RULE resulted from the two Old French words *reille* and *riule,* both from the Latin *regula,* a "straight" piece of wood, a RULER. The two French forms arose from a shift of accent in the Latin word. The pronunciation *re'gula* produced the French form *reille*, but when the word was pronounced *regu'la*, the French word developed as *riule*. REGULATE is from a Late Latin *regulare*, to make "straight," to make REGULAR. An iron RAIL is a "straight" bar of steel, a RULE or RULER retains the meaning of *regula*, while to RULE and to REGULATE both mean "to keep things *straight*."

RAVINE-RAPINE. RAVINE is a French word meaning first "a mountain torrent or raging flood" and then "a gully or RAVINE" through which the flood passes. The word goes back to the Latin *rapina*, plunder, pillage, RAPINE. So simply can two words stray so far apart in meaning! RAVISH is a related word and means "to seize and carry away with violence" or figuratively "to carry away with delight."

REVEL-REBEL. REVEL comes through Old French *reveler*, to riot, from the Latin *re-bellare*, to wage war again, to REBEL, formed on the noun *bellum*, war, a corruption of *duellum*, duel. The word "riot" connotes both "war" (or a disturbance approaching it) and REVELRY.

REVIEW-REVISE. REVIEW is an English form of the French *revue*, the past participle of the verb *revoir*, to see again, from Latin *re-videre*, to look at again. REVISE is from the past participle of this Latin verb, *re-visus*. The meanings of both words derive from the idea of "looking again at" the matter to be REVIEWED or REVISED.

SAVAGE-SILVAN. SAVAGE is from the Old French *salvage* (now *sauvage*), from a Late Latin adjective *silvaticus*, pertaining to a "forest" (*silva*) — see FOREST, page 47. A SAVAGE is a dweller in a "forest," while SILVAN, deriving directly from Latin *silva*, has the same meaning as the old *silvaticus*.

SPICE-SPECIES. SPICE is the Old French *espice*, spice, from the Latin *species*, kind, species. SPECIES, like PREMISE, was a medieval term of logic with a sense similar to the biological meaning of the word, as when we speak of the various SPECIES of plants or animals. The "spicers" (*épicier* is the French for "grocer") of the Middle Ages adopted the popular form of the word, SPICE, and applied it to the four "kinds" of things they had for sale: cloves, cinnamon, nutmegs, and saffron.

STRANGE-EXTRANEOUS. STRANGE came to us from Old French *estrange*, which was derived from the Latin *extraneus*, what is "outside," foreign, STRANGE. EXTERIOR is a related word. The word "foreign" (see page 47) brings STRANGE and EXTRANEOUS together — "foreign lands" are STRANGE lands and "foreign matter" is EXTRANEOUS matter.

TAVERN-TABERNACLE. TAVERN is the French *taverne*, tavern, inn, from Latin *taberna*, shed, booth, shop, inn. TABERNACLE comes from the diminutive *tabernaculum*, tent, literally "a little shed." The sacred associations of the word derive from its biblical use.

ZEST-SCHISM. The French *zeste* means "lemon peel" and so arise the ideas of "spicy flavor" and "keen enjoyment" contained in our use of ZEST. The French meaning was transferred from an older sense of "the *dividing skin* of the walnut," and the word goes back to the Greek *skhizein*, to divide, to split, whence also the word SCHISM. A SCHISM is specifically a "split" in the Church.

In addition to doublets which have come to us on the one hand from Old French and on the other from Latin, there are others coming either from two different forms of an Old French word, or from an Old French word and its modern equivalent. Both members of such pairs are usually "popular" words which have changed considerably in the course of their development throughout the centuries.

From Old French are derived both members of such doublets as the following:

FEEBLE-FOIBLE. Old French had the two forms *feble* and *foible*, both meaning "weak" and coming from the Latin *flebilis*, tearful. The form *foible* won out in French but has now become *faible*. A FOIBLE is precisely a "weakness."

LACE-LATCH. The Old French forms were *laz* and *lache*,

lace, from the Latin *laqueus,* noose, net, rope. Compare our use of "shoe LACE" and "LATCH string." Our LATCHES no longer have strings, although a friend of mine has ingeniously so arranged one on the door of his summer cottage. LASSO stems from *lazo,* the Spanish form of the same word.

PAY-APPEASE. PAY is from Old French *paier,* coming from Latin *pacare,* to make peace, to APPEASE. This verb was formed on the noun *pax,* PEACE. APPEASE is an Old French compound of *à,* to, and *pais,* peace, also from *pax.* When you PAY an installment on a debt, you do thereby APPEASE your debtor!

SLANDER-SCANDAL. In Old French we find the two forms *esclandre* and *escandle,* from a Late Latin *scandalum,* deriving from the Greek *skandalon,* snare. From *esclandre* we get SLANDER and from *escandle,* SCANDAL. These two words are closely associated in sense. The letters *l* and *r* are often substituted one for the other. We have seen such examples as GLAMOUR and GRAMMAR. Similarly, when the Latin *prunum* was early introduced into Anglo-Saxon, the word became PLUM. PRUNE is a later derivative from the Latin. In the same way, PURPLE has developed from the Anglo-Saxon form *purpure* which came from Latin *purpura.* The French equivalent *pourpre* has retained the *r.*

SQUAD-SQUARE. The Old French *esquadre* was borrowed from the Italian *squadra,* square, and the French form remained similar to the Italian original. Old French *esquarre,* square, developed regularly from the Latin *ex-quadra,* square, something having "four" sides, from *quatuor,* four. A SQUAD was originally a band of soldiers in a SQUARE formation. SQUADRON is from the Italian *squadrone,* a big SQUARE or "band" of men.

Such examples as BLAME-BLASPHEME and DAINTY-DIGNITY have all the earmarks of belonging to the group of French-Latin doublets, for the second member of each pair closely resembles its Latin original. In both cases, however, the doublets originated in Old French: *blasmer-blasfemer,* from a Late Latin *blasphemare* which goes back to the Greek *blasphemos,* evil speaking; and *dainté-digneté,* from Latin *dignitas,* worth, dignity, excellence. The meanings of BLAME and BLASPHEME derive easily from "evil speaking," and DIGNITY retains an original Latin sense. The idea behind DAINTY is: excellent — choice — delicious. Both BLASPHEME and DIGNITY owe their modern dress (and the close resemblance to their Latin and Greek originals) to spelling reforms introduced into both English and French by pedants of the XVIth century. In their enthusiasm for the classics they tried to make our words conform as much as possible to the original Latin and Greek spelling. The result was not a happy one.

Thus the Anglo-French word *receite* became RECEIPT, *dette* was changed to DEBT, *doute* to DOUBT, *enditer* to INDICT and *vitailles* to VICTUALS! By analogy with "science" they even manufactured SCISSORS and SCENT, whose Latin originals never had this initial *sc-*. SCISSORS is the Anglo-French *cisoires,* from Latin *cisorium,* a cutting instrument, and goes back ultimately to the verb *caedere,* to "cut down," to fell, to slay. The blunder in this spelling of SCISSORS arose through confusion with the Latin *scissus,* past participle of *scindere,* to cut, to divide. SCENT is the Middle English "sent," from the Anglo-French verb *sentir,* to smell, to feel (Latin *sentire*).

In many cases these inserted consonants even came to be pronounced in the course of time, and so we have PREGNABLE for the earlier *prenable,* PULSE for *pous,* FAULT for *faute,* MOULT for *mout,* PERFECT for *parfit,* SUBJECT for *subiet,* VERDICT for *veirdit* ("truly said"), and LANGUAGE for *langage.* An *h* was added to HABIT, HONOR, HOSPITAL, and HUMBLE. In none of these words was this *h* pronounced before the XIXth century. The *h* of HONOR is still silent while that of HUMBLE is uncertain. The blunder of the *d* in ADVANCE and ADVANTAGE was perhaps the most ludicrous of all. The error came about through analogy with such words as ADVENT and ADVENTURE which begin with the Latin prefix *ad-*, to. The Anglo-French *avancer* and *avantage*, however, went back to the Latin *ab-*, away, and *ante*, before (together forming *abante*). The *av-* of *avancer* and *avantage* is the Latin prefix *ab*. The authors of the revision, not recognizing the derivation of the words, took the initial *a-* for the Latin *ad-* and the result was etymological nonsense.

When we come to doublets derived, one from Old French, the other from modern French, we find that French too has not remained static since the Norman conquest of England. Some words that we took over have become obsolete in French, and others have changed considerably, both in spelling and in pronunciation. Indeed our spelling and pronunciation of these borrowed words often shows quite clearly whether they were from the language of the Norman invaders or whether we have borrowed them in more recent times. Another factor affecting the pronunciation of words taken from French since about the middle of the XVIIth century is the fad, which developed around that time, of pronouncing French words as nearly as possible *à la française*.

Thus we find, for instance, that words borrowed from modern French tend to keep the accent on the last syllable, giving such pairs as: GENTLE-GENTEEL, PREMIER-PREMIERE, GAL'LANT-GALLANT', and ANTIC-ANTIQUE. (ANTIC was first an adjective and then a noun, the sense developing thus: old — old-fashioned — quaint — queer — funny — funny action.) Other examples of this same French accent are: MASSAGE (as opposed to MESSAGE, an older word), PRESTIGE, MIRAGE, and GARAGE. Note also the pronunciation of the letter *g* (as between MASSAGE and MESSAGE, for example, the latter word showing the Old French pronunciation of *g*).

DEPLOY is the French *déployer*, while DISPLAY is from *despleier*, the Old French form of the word. DEPLOY, however, came into English fairly early, as is evident from the pronunciation of the *oy*, which had this sound in Old French. In the French of today *oy* and *oi* have the sound of "wa," as in *au revoir.* JOY, POISE, ANNOY, and OYSTER likewise came over into English before this sound shift took place in French. Old French *enoier* and *oistre* have now progressed still further to *ennuyer* (whence our borrowed noun ENNUI) and *huître*, which now has a quite superfluous *h*.

The pronunciation of *ch* is another indication of how long a French word has been in our language. Compare, for example, CHANDLER and CHANDELIER, CHAPEL and CHAPERON, CHIEF and CHEF. The Old French *ch* has become *sh* in French today, though the old spelling remains. Similarly, it is apparent that DETACH has been with us a long time while a military ATTACHÉ has not.

As we have seen (page 46), the letter *c* did not normally become *ch* in Norman French as it did in the speech of Paris. We therefore have MARKET, contrasting with the Central French *marché,* and CASTLE, from the early Norman *castel,* as opposed to CHATEAU, the Old French form of which was *chastel.* (MACKEREL came into English before this *-el* changed to *-eau* — the French word is now *maquereau.* We also have CAMEL, while the French equivalent is *chameau.*) This distinction between the Norman *c* and the Central French *ch* is not altogether reliable, however, for we also have such pairs as CAVALRY and CHIVALRY, CARESS and CHERISH, where the first member has not come from a Norman dialect, but was borrowed by the French from Italian. Thus CAVALRY is the French *cavallerie,* copied after the Italian *cavalleria,* whereas CHIVALRY comes from the Old French *chevalerie,* which developed regularly from the Late Latin *caballeria.* CAVALIER is also a French borrowing from the Italian *cavaliere.* CARESS was taken over by the French from the Italian noun *carezza,* a caress, while CHERISH is from the French verb *chérir.* Both go back to the Latin *carus,* dear.

Another strictly Norman form shows up in such examples as WAGE-GAGE, WARD-GUARD, and the compounds REWARD-REGARD. This *w* is of Germanic origin and was retained in Norman

French. In Parisian French the *w* changed to *g* or *gu*. Other examples are: WARRANTY and GUARANTY, WAR and the French *guerre,* WAIT and its Old French equivalent *gaite,* a sentinel, whence the modern French word *guetter,* to lie in WAIT for. WISE and GUISE provide the same contrast, but in this case WISE seems to have come directly from Anglo-Saxon rather than from a Germanic source through Norman French.

The "fitz" of FITZGERALD ("the son of Gerald") gives us another interesting sound shift from Old French. This FITZ is the French *fils,* son, now pronounced "feece." In Old French this word was pronounced "fitz." Similarly, the *c* of the Old French *groucier,* to murmur, was pronounced "ts." The old pronunciation "grootsiay" developed into "grootchiay," which gave a noun "grutch." This word later became GRUDGE.

Many French words have suffered a loss of consonants since the Battle of Hastings. This applies especially to the letter *s,* but some other consonants have been dropped too. In the second member of MEDLEY-MÊLÉE, the *d* is gone; in CORPSE-CORPS, the *s* remains in spelling but is not pronounced; in HOSTEL-HOTEL and FEAST-FÊTE, the *s* has disappeared.

FAINT-FEINT gives us still another example of a word borrowed twice from French. FAINT came to us from Old French and was the past participle of the verb *faindre,* to feign, to pretend. In modern French the verb is spelled *feindre,* and the noun derived from it is *feinte,* pretense, FEINT. The French has retained the meaning which we give to this later borrowing. FAINT has taken quite a different course in English. Woman's propensity to swoon was, at least in the past, in large part FEIGNED. The first meaning of FAINT was, therefore, "to *pretend* to lose consciousness." Later man became a little less skeptical. From the sense of "swoon" has developed that of "weak," which we give to the adjective.

Now that we have taken up the doublets which have come to us either directly from Latin or indirectly by way of French, there remain a few interesting examples from other sources.

From Latin through French and Italian we have received the doublets COWARD-CODA and PORCH-PORTICO. PORCH and PORTICO are the French and Italian forms of the Latin word *porticus,* porch. COWARD is from the Old French *coart* which meant both "hare" and COWARD, the latter meaning arising from the well-known timidity of Br'er Rabbit. The literal meaning of *coart* was "the tailed one," and the word came from the Latin *cauda,* tail. CODA is an Italian word from the same source and means a "tail" attached to a piece of music.

From Latin by way of French and Spanish we have PIONEER and PEON. The French *pionnier* was formed on *pion,* from the Latin *pedonem,* foot soldier (from *pedem,* foot). The Spanish *peón* has the same derivation.

From Latin through French and Portuguese we have borrowed such different words as MATTER and MADEIRA. MATTER comes through Old French *matere* from the Latin *materia,* MATTER, MATERIAL, and especially "timber." The last meaning gave its name to the Portuguese island of MADEIRA, from which comes the wine of the same name. The island was so-called because it was heavily covered with "timber."

From Latin directly, and through Italian, come DICTUM and DITTO. The Latin *dictum,* meaning "a thing said," was the past participle of the verb *dicere,* to say. A DICTUM is "a thing said" dogmatically, while DITTO, an Italian word, refers to "a thing said" before.

From Latin through French and Hungarian are derived CORSAIR and HUSSAR. CORSAIR is a French word, from a Late Latin *cursarius,* runner, formed on the verb *currere,* to run. HUSSAR wandered far in the opposite direction. This word is the Hungarian *huszar,* borrowed from the Serbian *husar,* a corruption of the Italian *corsaro,* from the same Latin *cursarius.*

From Latin through French and Dutch have come CROSS and CRUISE. CROSS is from the Old French *crois,* derived from the Latin *crux,* cross. From Old French the word went over into Dutch and became the verb *kruisen,* from which we get

CRUISE. Both words get their meanings from the "criss-cross" movement of sailing ships.

From Greek through French and German we get SLAVE and SLAV. SLAVE is from the French *esclave,* derived from a Late Latin *sclavus,* a "Slavic" captive, from the Greek *Sklabos,* SLAV. The word SLAV itself came through the German *Sklave* from the same Greek word.

From Arabic directly, and by way of French, we have received SHRUB and SYRUP. This SHRUB is not the word that means "bush." I do not believe I have heard the word used elsewhere than at home, but when I was a boy my mother each year made quantities of raspberry SHRUB, strawberry SHRUB, etc. The result was a fruit SYRUP, later to be thinned with water to make a strictly unfermented Methodist drink. This word SHRUB comes from the Arabic *sharab*, drink, cordial. SYRUP has come from the same source, through the French form *sirop.*

From Turkish directly, and through French, came TURBAN and TULIP. TURBAN is from the Turkish *tulbend,* TURBAN. The French form *tulipe* comes from an earlier *tulipan,* also from *tulbend.* The TULIP is a "TURBAN-like" flower.

From German by way of French and Dutch, are derived BOULEVARD and BULWARK, SKIFF and SKIPPER, and WAFER and WAFFLE. The French word BOULEVARD is from the German *Bollwerk,* bulwark, fortification, literally "log-work." The present use of BOULEVARD arises from the building of the BOULE-VARDS of Paris on the site of old "fortifications" which had ringed the city. BULWARK comes directly from the Dutch form *bolwerk.* SKIFF is from the French *esquif* which seems to have come from the German *skif*, ship. SKIPPER is the Dutch *schipper* (Dutch *sch = sk*), from *schip,* ship. The word SHIP itself is obviously related, but was already present in Anglo-Saxon. EQUIP is another related word, coming from the French *équiper.* This French word came from an Old Norse *skipa,* to man a ship, and was brought to France by the "Northmen." WAFER is from the Old French *waufre,* from German *wafel,* wafer. WAFFLE comes directly from the Dutch *wafel.*

From German directly, and through French, come ROB and ROBE. ROB is from the Old German *roubon,* to rob (now *rauben*). ROBE is an Old French word which goes back to the Old German noun *roub,* booty, and especially booty in the form of a "garment" — a ROBE.

Returning to Latin, we find two interesting doublets which come from Latin through Anglo-Saxon and French: INCH-OUNCE and SILK-SERGE. The word INCH is particularly interesting because it is probably the oldest word in our language derived from Latin. The Germanic tribes borrowed this word from Latin before the invasion of England by the Angles and Saxons. The Anglo-Saxon form was *ynce,* from the Latin *uncia,* a twelfth part. OUNCE is a much later borrowing, from the Old French *unce,* and in troy weight an OUNCE is still a "twelfth part" of a pound. SILK is from the Anglo-Saxon *seoloc,* which looks like a very bad attempt of a primitive people to pronounce the Latin word *serica,* silks, silken garments. This word in turn came from *Seres,* the Chinese, a people famed for their silken fabrics. The Old French *serge* also developed from *serica.*

Another curious Anglo-Saxon corruption of a Latin word was *lopustra* for the Latin *locusta. Lopustra* has now become LOBSTER. The Latin word meant both LOCUST and LOBSTER.

Finally, there are a few doublets deriving from Anglo-Saxon and Scandinavian. Because these are of less interest, I shall confine myself to one example: ROAD and RAID. RAID is a Scandinavian form equivalent to the Anglo-Saxon *rad,* ROAD, formed from *ridan,* to ride. The word "inroad" serves to link the two words in meaning, for an "inroad" is a RAID.

Chapter VIII

THE GREEKS HAD A WORD FOR IT

THROUGHOUT the preceding chapters we have seen many words that have come to us from Greek and Latin originals. Some of these derivations were readily recognizable while others had been well camouflaged. There are also in English many words which we have taken over bodily from Greek and Latin, without even changing a letter of the original orthography. We saw a few such words in the last chapter: MOMENTUM, CAMERA, PASTOR.

From Greek we have words like ANATHEMA, "an accursed thing," AROMA, "spice," ASBESTOS, "inextinguishable," ASTHMA, "a panting," DOGMA, "opinion," HOI POLLOI, "the many," IDEA, "look" (from the verb *idein,* to see), MANIA "madness," and PATHOS, "suffering."

Likewise from Greek, with very minor changes, are ASPARAGUS, from *aspharagos,* "asparagus;" CACTUS, from *kaktos,* "a prickly plant;" CRATER, from *krater,* "mixing bowl;" EUREKA, from *heureka,* "I have found;" and NECTAR, from *nektar,* "drink of the gods."

When we come to Latin, there are such obvious forms as EX OFFICIO, HABEAS CORPUS, and STATUS QUO, which most people at once recognize as Latin words, even if they do not know their meaning.

On the other hand, there are a great many very common words which most of us do not normally think of as Latin terms, even though we may have been exposed to Caesar, Cicero, and Virgil. In this category I would place such words as ALIBI, "elsewhere;" AREA, "open field;" ARENA, "sand" (the ARENAS of ancient times were strewn with sand); BONUS, "good;" CAMPUS, "field;" CIRCUS, "circle," "ring," and then "a large oval enclosure for races, etc.;" DELIRIUM, "madness" (see

DELIRIOUS, page 68); DIPLOMA, "official paper," literally "a paper folded *double* (from the Greek *diploos*, double);" ECHO, "echo" (going back to the Greek *ekho*, sound); ERROR, "a wandering" (from *errare*, to wander, and hence to ERR); FACTOR, "maker," "doer;" FAVOR, "favor," "good-will;" FOCUS, "hearth;" FUROR, "madness;" HERNIA, "rupture;" HONOR, "respect;" HORROR, "great fear;" HUMOR, "fluid" (see page 77); INDEX, "informer," "discloser," "index;" SECTOR, "cutter" (see INSECT, page 55); INTERIOR, "inner;" JUNIOR and SENIOR, "younger" and "older;" LABOR, "work;" LATEX, "liquid" (in English, the "liquid" or juice of the rubber tree); LENS, "lentil" (because a double convex lens has the shape of a lentil); MICA, "crumb," "little piece" (if you have seen rocks covered with "bits" of MICA, you will readily understand this transfer); MILITIA, "soldiery;" MISER, "wretched," "MISERable;" MOTOR, "one who moves;" NAUSEA, "shipsickness" (from the Greek *naus*, ship — compare NAUTICAL); ODOR, "smell;" OPERA, "work;" POLLEN, "something sifted," "fine flour," "dust;" PUS, "pus;" RECTOR, "ruler" (from *rectus*, the past participle of *regere*, to rule — see RULE and REGULATE, page 97); RUMOR, "hearsay."

We have one group of adjectives that have been altered only by the insertion of an *o* in the Latin originals: ERRONEOUS, from *erroneus*, "straying;" FATUOUS, from *fatuus*, "foolish;" FRIVOLOUS, from *frivolus*, "trifling;" GARRULOUS, from *garrulus*, "chattering;" MISCELLANEOUS, from *miscellaneus,* "miscellaneous;" NEFARIOUS, from *nefarius*, "impious;" NOTORIOUS, from *notorius*, "publicly known," "noted;" OBNOXIOUS, from *obnoxius*, "harmful;" PRECARIOUS, from *precarius*, "obtained by prayer (from *precari*, to pray)," "doubtful;" RAUCOUS, from *raucus*, "hoarse;" and RIDICULOUS, from *ridiculus*, "laughable."

We have taken over several Latin gerundives: ADDENDUM, something "to be added," from *addere*, to add; AGENDA, things "to be done," from *agere*, to do; MEMORANDUM, something "to be remembered," from *memorare*, to recall; REFERENDUM, something "to be referred," from *referre*, to carry back, to

REFER. The proper names AMANDA and MIRANDA mean literally "one to be loved," from *amare*, to love, and "one to be admired," from *admirari*, to admire.

DATA means "things given" and is the plural of *datum*, the past participle of the Latin verb *dare*, to give. DONATION comes from the related *donationem*.

We have come to use as nouns an odd assortment of Latin parts of speech, as is evident from such examples as ITEM, QUORUM, and POSSE. ITEM was an adverb in Latin and meant "likewise" or "also." The word came to be used in making out lists, as for example: butter, ITEM ("also") cheese, ITEM ("also") milk, ITEM ("also") eggs, etc. Gradually the sense was transferred to the ITEMS of the list. QUORUM is the Latin plural pronoun "whose," and refers to the number of persons "whose" presence is necessary to transact business. POSSE is an abbreviation of the Medieval Latin phrase *posse comitatus*, "the power of the county." In Classical Latin *posse* was the infinitive "to be able," but in Late Latin times the word had already come to be used as a noun with the sense of "power."

The most curious examples of this substitution of one part of speech for another are Latin finite verb forms which we now use as nouns. In the first person singular we have CREDO, "I believe," and VETO, "I forbid;" in the second person, such commands as DIRGE (a shortening of *dirige*, "direct thou" — *dirige* is the first word of a Latin hymn used in Catholic services for the dead), HABEAS CORPUS, "take the body," MEMENTO, "remember thou," and RECIPE, "receive thou;" in the third person singular: AFFIDAVIT, "he has pledged," DEFICIT, "it is lacking," FIAT, "let it be done," HABITAT, "it dwells," INTEREST, "it matters," literally "it is between" (from *inter-esse*, to be between — to be apart, with a space "between" — to be different — to make a difference — to matter), and TENET, "he holds;" in the first person plural: IGNORAMUS, "we do not know," and the legal "writs" of MANDAMUS, "we command," and MITTIMUS, "we send" (a writ of MANDAMUS directs or commands somebody to do a certain thing, and a writ of MITTIMUS is a warrant "committing" a person to prison); and in the third person plural, the word DEBENTURE (Latin *debentur*), "are due." Used as the first word in a voucher, *debentur* meant "(the following items) are due."

To conclude our discussion of the Latin element in English, let us take a glance at a few of the mongrel words which we have manufactured from various combinations of Latin and Anglo-Saxon derivatives.

First we have combinations of Anglo-Saxon words and Latin prefixes, such as ANTEROOM, from Latin *ante-*, before, and "room;" COWORKER, from Latin *con-*, with, and "worker;" DE-HORN, from Latin *de-*, away, and "horn;" DISLIKE, from Latin *dis-*, not, and "like;" and INTERMINGLE, from Latin *inter-*, among, and "mingle."

Anglo-Saxon words have also been combined with Latin suffixes, and we get words like BREAKAGE, from "break" and the Latin *-aticum* (through Old French *-age*); READABLE, from "read" and Latin *-a-bilis;* STARVATION, from "starve" — which originally meant "to die" and then "to die of hunger," and which has its counterpart in the German *sterben,* to die — and Latin *-a-tion;* and TALKATIVE, from "talk" and Latin *-a-tivus.*

Then, by way of contrast, we find Latin words combined with old Anglo-Saxon prefixes and suffixes. First a few examples of combinations with prefixes: BECAUSE, from "by" — the word was once spelled "bicause" — and Latin *causa,* cause; UNJUST, from "un-" and Latin *justus,* right; FORETASTE, from "fore-" and Old French *taster;* and OVERCHARGE, from "over" and Old French *charger.*

Turning to Latin words combined with native suffixes, we find such examples as BEAUTIFUL, from Old French *beauté* and "-ful;" COMPANIONSHIP, from Old French *compaignon* and "-ship;" FALSEHOOD, from Latin *falsus* and "-hood;" and VEN-TURESOME, from Old French (*a*)*venture* and "some."

In addition to such combinations with prefixes and suffixes, there are examples of whole Anglo-Saxon and Latin words compounded, such as FAINTHEARTED, from Old French *faint* and "heart," and HEIRLOOM, from Old French *heir* and "loom."

Finally, we should not leave the subject of mongrel words without looking at the masterpiece MACADAMIZATION, which manages to combine four languages: MAC (Gaelic) ADAM (Hebrew) -IZ (Greek) -ATION (Latin).

Chapter IX

ONE WORLD

WE MAY picture the world as a great human ant-hill, with men swarming all over it, back and forth, hither and yon, across land and sea, carrying with them not only goods and war and the Word of God, but also words, words, always words. Whether they were traders, soldiers, or missionaries, they had to try as best they could to make themselves understood by the foreign peoples with whom they came in contact. This intercourse worked both ways, and travellers not only left many of their own words among foreigners, to be later adopted and used, but also brought strange words back home, where they became a part of the native speech.

With the advent of air travel our language is bound to become even more cosmopolitan than it now is. Our soldiers, who have been quartered in every part of the world, are bringing back all kinds of strange words, many of which will find their way into our speech. Indeed, think of the foreign terms which have become commonplace to the man in the street, simply from reading and hearing about World War II, words which he had certainly never heard before. Now he

can reel off many German and Japanese words as glibly as if
he had known them from birth. Quite aside from strange and
exotic place names, we have become quite familiar with such
Japanese words as *banzai, samurai,* and *kamikaze,* while we
could almost make an *ersatz* language from our new German
vocabulary: *Nazi, Führer* (and *duce,* its Italian counterpart),
Gestapo, Blitzkrieg (and *blitz*-everything-else), *Luftwaffe,*
Panzer, Autobahn. While our man in the street may still find
Lebensraum and *Drang nach Osten* too much of a mouthful,
he certainly has been exposed to these words often enough.

We have seen in Chapter I how our language got its start
from the wanderings of primitive Indo-European tribes, and
how the original speech of Britain was completely eclipsed by
successive invasions and occupations of foreign armies and
peoples. We have seen the influence of the Crusades, when
returning soldiers and pilgrims brought back many words
from the East. We have seen how early traders brought words
from the Far and Near East by way of France, because in
early times the dangers and difficulties of long voyages by
sea were too great; and how, with the rise of the British
Empire and the accompanying increase in trade with the four
corners of the earth, many exotic terms were introduced into
our tongue.

In the succeeding chapters we have found other words
which have come into English by more or less devious routes,
notably words of Germanic origin which have come by way
of France. Some of these came very early into Latin from
German tribesmen who fought in the Roman armies. Others
came with the successive invasions of France by the Franks,
Goths, and Burgundians, while a few more were introduced
after the later invasion of the "Northmen." We find a few such
words of Germanic origin which we have not met before:
BIVOUAC, a French word deriving from the German *Beiwache,*
extra night guard; ROAST, through Old French *rostir,* from the
German verb *rosten* (formed on the noun *Rost,* grate); TOWEL,

through Old French *toaille*, from the Germanic *twahila*, a cloth for washing or wiping (from *twahan*, to wash); and VENEER, which actually came to us directly from German, but which has wandered back and forth across the Franco-German frontier. This word starts with an Old German adjective *frum*, excellent. (The modern form is *fromm*, which has also assumed the meanings of "pious" and "innocent.") From this adjective was formed the verb *frumman*, to make excellent, to improve, and then "to furnish." With this meaning, the word was borrowed by the French in Late Latin times, with the form *fornire* which developed into Old French *fornir* and then into the modern *fournir*, from which comes our English FURNISH. The Germans then re-borrowed the French *fournir* to make the German verb *fournieren*, to furnish. From this verb was formed the noun *Fournier*, used first for "inlay" and then for VENEER. Frederick the Great of Prussia was a great admirer of everything French, and his influence was responsible for introducing into German a large number of French words. German nationalists have been trying ever since to "purify" their language, but have not been altogether successful in eliminating these French words from the German vocabulary.

Many well-travelled words show how ancient civilization was concentrated in the Mediterranean area, and how words were carried back and forth across and around this inland sea.

Thus SUGAR originated in India with the Old Sanskrit word *çarkara*, came into ancient Persia in the form of *shakar* (see SEERSUCKER, page 25), was taken over as *sakkar* by the Arabs who introduced the word into Spain, where it became *azucar*. The French borrowed this Spanish word, changing it to *sucre*, from which we got our own form of the word. But the Arabic *sakkar* also went around the other end of the Mediterranean into Greece, to form the word *sakkharon*, which we have borrowed to describe SACCHARIN, the sugar substitute.

In Greek the word CARAT was *keration*, which meant originally "the seed of the carob tree," an evergreen growing in the region of the Mediterranean. This Greek word became the Arabic *qirat,* from which the Italians formed *carato.* The French borrowed their *carat* from Italy and then took it across the Channel to England.

The Greeks took *elephantos* from an ancient Egyptian word. The Romans borrowed it from Greece, with the characteristic change from *o* to *u,* in the form of *elephantus.* The word occurred in Old French as *olifant,* but was later changed to *éléphant* to conform with the Latin spelling. Our ELEPHANT was in turn borrowed from French.

Similarly, the Greeks borrowed *kamelos* from the Hebrew *gamal.* The Romans took the word from Greek as *camelus,* which ultimately gave us CAMEL.

The word APRICOT comes from Latin, but by a very roundabout route. APRICOT starts from the Latin *praecoccia,* a corrupted form of *praecoqua,* "early ripe" or PRECOCIOUS, from *prae,* early, and *coquere,* to cook, to ripen. (KITCHEN is from this same word, which entered very early into Anglo-Saxon.) The Latin *praecoccia* was then borrowed by the Greeks, bucking the almost exclusively one-way traffic of Greek words into Latin. The Arabs took the Greek form *praikokia* and made of it *al burquq* (see ALFALFA, etc., page 40), which they introduced into Spain, where it became *albaricoque.* From Spain the word returned to Italy in the form of *albricocco,* and thus completed a Cook's tour of the Mediterranean. The French in turn borrowed their *abricot* from either Italian or Spanish and took it with them to England, where the English reinserted the Latin *p* to form APRICOT.

In the foregoing chapters we have seen words like RAIL, which came from a French word, and which the French have re-borrowed in the English form and with the English meaning. We have also observed REDINGOTE and MOIRE, which were English words, borrowed by the French, and later taken back into English with their French dress and meaning. There are many English words of French origin which came to England

on a round-trip ticket, good for several hundred years. Thus
BUDGET came from the Old French *bougette,* a little bag
(BULGE has the same derivation, from Latin *bulga,* bag), but
the French now balance their *budgets.* FASHION is from the
Old French *façon,* manner, way, but the French now like to
be *fashionable* by keeping up with *les fashions!* We borrowed
INTERVIEW from the Old French *entrevue* and REPORTER from
the French verb *reporter,* to carry back; but now in France a
reporter may *interviewer* a celebrity just as in the U. S. A.
JURY came from the Old French *jurée,* oath, but French crim-
inals are now tried before a *jury.* SPORT is a shortened form of
DISPORT, from the Old French *se desporter,* literally "to carry
oneself apart," to amuse oneself, but the French game of *foot-
ball* is now a *sport.* TOURIST is from TOUR, which came from
the French *tourner,* to turn, but the French will never be
happy until *les touristes* return, and the business of *tourisme*
is resumed.

In order to see what a truly varied assortment of words we
do have in our language, and from what a variety of sources
they have come, let us start south from England on a trip
around the world. We may skip France, whose contribution
to our language we already know, and go directly to Italy,
from which we have such words as FIASCO, IMBROGLIO,
INCOGNITO, LAVA, and LIBRETTO, not to mention many other
musical terms.

From Italy, crossing over to Spain and Portugal, we have
from Portuguese such words as CASTE, used by them in reference to the Hindus (the Portuguese were the first colonizers
of India), and YAM, which the Portuguese took from Africa.
From Spain we get words like ARMADA, EMBARGO, FIESTA,
FLOTILLA, LOCO, and SILO.

From the Spanish peninsula we cross the Straits of Gib-
raltar and come to the Arabs of North Africa. From Arabic
have come CIPHER (the Italians borrowed the same word and
and made ZERO out of it), GIRAFFE, LILAC, SASH, SOFA, and TALC.

Continuing around the Mediterranean, we come to Turkey, which has given us such different words as HORDE, from Turkish *orda,* the first meaning of which was "camp" (wandering tribes living in tents), the interjection BOSH!, a Turkish word meaning "empty," and DIVAN, which meant first "privy council," then "council hall," and later "sofa in a council hall." This word goes back to the Persian *diwan,* tribunal, council.

Turning south for other Persian words, we find BAZAAR, CARAVAN, PAJAMA (Persian *pay,* leg, and *jamah,* clothing), and SHAWL. The words CHESS and CHECK(-mate) go back to the Persian *shah,* king (see EX-CHEQUER, page 59), and the chess term ROOK is from the Persian *rukh,* castle.

Across the Arabian Sea from Persia lies India, and from here we have such words as LOOT, SHAMPOO, and TOM-TOM. Most people would expect the latter word to have come from Africa.

East of India is the Malay Peninsula, and here we have picked up words like ATOLL (which few of us had heard of before the war in the Pacific), KAPOK, SAGO, and TEAK.

On the path across the Pacific between Malaya and Australia lie the islands of Polynesia, from which have come TATTOO and TABOO, while from Australia itself we have the native word KANGAROO.

Continuing on to South America, we find such native South American Indian words as JAGUAR, GAUCHO, and PAMPAS, which have been adopted by the Spanish to the south of us.

From Mexico some Spanish words have come into our Southwest, as, for example, BRONCO and COYOTE.

Now that we have reached the borders of the United States, we may note such North American Indian words as PECAN, SKUNK, TOBOGGAN, and SQUASH, after which, if we wish, we may continue on and find our way back to England by a northern route.

If we stop in Alaska, we find the Alaskan Indian word HOOCH and the Eskimo term KAYAK.

Going on to Asia, through Japan and China, we pick up

the Japanese KIMONO and TYCOON ("a great prince") and the Chinese TEA and KOWTOW.

From China we proceed north again through Siberia to Russia, where we have borrowed KNOUT, MAMMOTH (this is the Russian name for the huge extinct elephant-like animal, fossils of which have been found in both North America and Siberia — from this name is our adjective MAMMOTH derived), POGROM ("devastation"), and UKASE.

Westward from Russia, across the Baltic, we come to Scandinavia, where we find the Norwegian SKI, the Swedish DANK ("a marshy place") and LUG ("to pull the hair," from *lugg*, forelock), and the Danish SCOWL and SHY.

South from Denmark lies Germany which has given us such words as DOLLAR, CONCERTMEISTER (now usually further anglicized to CONCERTMASTER), KINDERGARTEN, LIEDER, not to mention SAUERKRAUT.

And finally we return to England by way of Holland, whose close ties with the British Isles have produced DAPPER ("brave," the same word as the German *tapfer*), DRILL (ultimately from the same source as THRILL — see page 58), GROOVE ("furrow"), GRUFF ("coarse"), HOLSTER, LANDSCAPE, and SPOOK ("ghost").

As the reader has doubtless observed, words borrowed from far-away places are usually nouns. When an English trader tries to make himself understood by a Hottentot, neither party is likely to go very deeply into matters of syntax. Such words are largely names of concrete objects and are apt to have been answers to "What is it?"

Chapter X

FOOTPRINTS IN THE SANDS OF TIME

In the last few years we have become familiar with names of far-away places which we had never heard of before. Even in our every-day speech, however, we have long used many such strange and exotic place-names without being aware of it. We have already seen, for example, that the names of most wines are really the names of the regions where these famous vintages are produced. The names of other commonplace things are similarly derived, not only from places scattered all over the globe, but also from people, who, in some way or other, have thus immortalized their names.

The latest and most obvious example of a word so bequeathed to us by an individual (though he could hardly have wished to attain immortality by this method) is QUISLING, which will doubtless forever be synonymous with "traitor." On the other hand, a BENEDICT is not necessarily a "traitor" to his former companions who prefer to remain in the state of single blessedness. This word comes, not from Benedict Arnold, the traitor of Revolutionary days, but from Shakespeare's hero Benedick in the play *Much Ado About Nothing*. This character scoffs at marriage but in the end succumbs.

We have already seen that the word BRAGGADOCIO also stems from a character in a play. Even stranger words that have come to us in this manner are PANTS and ZANY. PANTS is an abbreviation of "pantaloons." This word is the Italian *pantalone*, and in the Italian *commedia dell'arte* of the Middle Ages, *Pantalone* was the name of a stock character, a buffoon who wore the tight-fitting "pants" of the Venetians. Another stock character of this old Italian comedy was *Giovanni*, also a clown. This word the Italians corrupted to *zanni* from which, through the French form *zani*, we get ZANY, a clown.

Turning from "play actors" to actual people, we find such words as BOYCOTT, after Captain Boycott, an Irish land agent of the last century, and the first well-known victim of this strategy; MARTINET, from Martinet, a notorious drillmaster under Louis XIV; and SADISM, after the Comte de Sade, an XVIIIth century French writer of obscene stories. DUNCE is from John Duns Scotus, a famous scholar of the XIIIth century who was held up to ridicule for his opposition to progress in methods of learning. Even the word JACKANAPES takes us back to "Jack Napes," a nickname given early in the XVth century to William de la Pole, Duke of Suffolk, whose badge was a clog and chain, like that of a tame ape. "Jack Napes" was apparently short for "Jack of Naples," which would seem to have been a popular name for pet apes and monkeys. These were common in the Middle Ages and were imported into England from Italy.

Less spectacular perhaps are many articles, named for their inventors. The BLOOMER girls are named after a Mrs. Bloomer who about 1850 invented this outmoded article of feminine apparel. The RAGLAN sleeve was named after Lord Raglan who lived in England during the first half of the last century. Similarly, the DERBY hat was named for the Earl of Derby. The BOWIE knife was invented by Colonel James Bowie, an American pioneer and soldier; the MONKEY wrench, by Thomas Monkey; the SAXOPHONE, by A. J. Saxe; SHRAPNEL, by General Shrapnel of the British army; and the SPINET, by Giovanni Spinetti of Venice.

TIMOTHY grass was introduced into this country early in the XVIIIth century by Timothy Hanson. NICOTINE was named after Monsieur Nicot, who first brought tobacco to France. GRAHAM flour was popularized during the first half of the last century by Sylvester Graham, an American writer on dietetics. The process of MERCERIZING cotton was perfected by J. Mercer. And our MACADAM roads are due to the efforts of J. L.

McAdam, a Scotch engineer who invented this process early in the XIXth century.

The electrical terms AMPERE, VOLT, and WATT are all named after early electrical researchers: André Marie Ampère of France, Alessandro Volta of Italy, and James Watt of Scotland (the inventor of the steam engine).

DERRICK, on the other hand, is named, not for its inventor, but for a XVIIth century English hangman named Derrick. The word first meant "hangman" but was later applied to the gibbet used for hanging.

Just as we have taken some words from names of characters in plays, so we have derived others from characters of ancient mythology. Thus ATLAS was the giant who held the world on his shoulders (actually, he was condemned to hold up the heavens); when we seal anything HERMETICALLY, we only make it air-tight, but the word derives from Hermes, the Greek god who presided over the "secrets" of science and philosophy; VOLCANO and VULCANIZE take us back to Vulcan, the Roman god of fire and the forge; while the adjectives JOVIAL, MER-CURIAL, and SATURNINE are named after the Roman gods Jupiter (a compound of *Jovis* and *pater*, meaning "Father Jove"), Mercury, and Saturn. These last three, however, have come to us indirectly through medieval astrology. Jupiter was the happiest star under which to be born, and its "influence" gave one a cheerful or JOVIAL disposition. The planet Mercury made one fickle or MERCURIAL, while Saturn gave you a gloomy or SATURNINE temperament.

The verb to TANTALIZE is from Tantalus, the bad boy of Greek mythology. This son of Zeus committed so many crimes that he was punished in the lower world by being placed in water up to his neck; then, whenever he stooped over to drink, the water receded and he was never able to quench his thirst. Or he was placed under a tree whose branches were heavily laden with fruit; but as he reached up to pluck the fruit, the branches invariably rose just beyond his grasp.

When we come to words derived from place names, we find that the names of most fabrics have originated from the locality where they were first manufactured. From the cities of Cambrai and Lille in Northern France have come CAMBRIC and LISLE. In Southern France POPLIN was manufactured in the "papal" city of Avignon — the French word is *popeline*. (In the XIVth century, during a schism in the Church, Avignon was the residence of the Pope.) We have seen (page 90) how DENIM came from Nîmes, another city of Southern France. CRETONNE and TULLE also originated in the French towns of Créton and Tulle.

Most of us now think of a DUFFEL bag as something to hold our DUFFEL, but in so doing we are putting the cart before the horse. While these bags are now usually made of duck rather than DUFFEL, this is the name of a heavy woolen material, first produced in the town of Duffel in Belgium. The bag got its name from the material of which it was made, and later the meaning of DUFFEL was transferred to the contents of the bag, usually camping supplies.

Our blue JEANS are made from a twilled cotton material that used to be called "jean." This word seems to go back to the city of Genoa in Italy, from which the material was brought to England. From England itself we get WORSTED, first made at the town of Worsted in Norfolk.

China's city of Nanking has given us NANKEEN, while CASHMERE and MADRAS first came from Kashmir and Madras in India.

From Syria the city of Damascus has given its name to DAMASK, and GAUZE was first produced at Gaza. Also from the Near East, we have MUSLIN, which came from Mosul in what is now known as Iraq, and, while ERMINE is hardly a fabric, this word came from Armenia.

The names of other materials show us their place of origin. AGATE is named for the Achates River in Sicily, near which this stone was first found. BRONZE is a relic of the Latin phrase (*aes*) *Brundisium,* (brass) of Brindisi, a town of Southern Italy. COPPER was formed in the same way, from the Latin (*aes*) *Cyprium,* (brass) of Cyprus, and MAGNESIA is from the Greek *Magnesia* (*lithos*), (stone) of Magnesia. MAGNET and MANGANESE are corruptions of the same word.

Among articles of clothing there are such obvious examples as OXFORDS, JERSEY, PANAMA, HOMBURG, and ULSTER, but few are aware of the origin of CRAVAT and TUXEDO. The French *cravate* means "Croatian," and neckties were first worn by Croat soldiers in the French army way back in 1636. TUXEDO, on the other hand, dates only from 1866, when Pierre Lorillard appeared at a ball in Tuxedo Park, New York, dressed in tail-less "tails," which he had had especially tailored. The new-fangled dress suit was at once dubbed TUXEDO, and both the suit and the name stuck.

Some of the things we eat are named after places where these foods originated. CANTALOUPES were first grown in Europe at Cantalupo in Italy. We have seen (page 90) how CURRANTS got their name from the city of Corinth in Greece. The French have named famous sauces after their places of origin: MAYONNAISE, from Mayonne, BORDELAISE, from Bordeaux, HOLLANDAISE, from Holland, etc. In the same way, TABASCO sauce is named for Tabasco in Mexico. Coming to something more substantial, we have SARDINES, from the Island of Sardinia, BOLOGNA, from the Italian city of the same name, HAMBURGERS, FRANKFURTERS, and WIENERS, from Hamburg, Frankfurt, and Vienna (spelled *Wien* in German). PHEASANTS were named after the Phasis River in Greece, and the origin of TURKEY needs no explanation, except to say that the word was first applied to guinea fowl, which were brought to Europe from Africa via Turkey.

There remains a miscellany of words thus derived from place names, including two verbs: MEANDER, from the winding River Maiandos in Asia Minor, and CANTER, from Canterbury, in allusion to the easy pace of pilgrims riding to the shrine of Thomas à Becket. As late as the XVIIIth century the expression "on the canterbury" meant "on the trot."

Several assorted words have come to us from Italy, of which the most obvious is ITALICS. It was in Italy in the year 1501 that the famous printer Aldus Manutius first introduced this variety of type. Many centuries earlier there stood on the "Palatine" Hill in Rome the PALACE of the Emperor Augustus. The word PISTOL comes from the Italian town of Pistoia. Originally a PISTOL was a particular type of dagger manufactured there. A MILLINER was once a "milaner," a dealer in goods from Milan — fancy wares, ribbons, etc. The TARANTULA spider is found especially in Southern Italy and was named after the town of Taranto.

BAYONETS were first made in the French town of Bayonne, down near the Spanish frontier, and the word VAUDEVILLE is a corruption of the French *Vau-de-Vire* (Valley of the Vire) in Normandy. This was the birthplace of the XVth century poet Basselin, a composer of gay songs.

Most of us in these days of apartment-house dwellers have forgotten what an ATTIC looks like, and few would ever associate one with ancient Greece. This word is nevertheless due to the fact that "Attic" buildings ("Attica" was the ancient country of Greece) were built with gable roofs and thus had an ATTIC space. It is interesting to observe that the synonym GARRET meant, in medieval France, "a watchtower." This word, as well as GARRISON, goes back to the Old French *garir*, to defend.

Finally, there is the expressive American word BUNK. This is an abbreviation of BUNKUM, which came from Buncombe County in North Carolina. The congressman from this district once made such an inane speech, in order to impress his constituents, that the name of Buncombe County spread like wildfire. The sense was originally restricted to "empty speech-making," but was later extended to any sort of "baloney."

Open Shelf Department

INDEX